MW01489576

SET US FREE

What the Church Needs to Know from Survivors of Abuse

Ann W. Annis
Michelle Loyd-Paige
Rodger R. Rice

Calvin College Social Research Center
and
University Press of America,® Inc.
Lanham · New York · Oxford

Copyright © 2001 by
University Press of America,® Inc.
4720 Boston Way
Lanham, Maryland 20706

12 Hid's Copse Rd.
Cumnor Hill, Oxford OX2 9JJ

Library of Congress Cataloging-in-Publication Data

Annis, Ann W.
Set us free : what the church needs to know from survivors
of abuse / Ann W. Annis, Michelle Loyd-Paige, Rodger R. Rice.
p.   cm
Includes bibliographical references and index.
1. Church work. I. Loyd-Paige, Michelle. II. Rice, Rodger R. III. Title.
BV4400 .A55   2000   261.8'32—dc21   00-048859 CIP

ISBN 0-7618-1905-3 (pbk. : alk. paper)

Dedication

To the over 200 survivors who responded to our media request for interviews, and especially the 67 who talked with us in depth for this project. We recognize the courage it took to talk of such personal and painful experiences with a complete stranger. A few of you persistently inquired of the project, urging us to complete our task. Because of your courage and encouragement, we dedicate this book to you.

Contents

Preface

Upon completion of a 1990 survey of the prevalence of abuse in the Christian Reformed Church, we began to formulate the idea of a project looking at the relationships among abuse, religion, and church. We felt it should consist of in-depth interviews of abuse survivors, so we could better explore their stories, their experiences. After meeting with and interviewing five survivors and two psychologists as resource people who helped us better define our project and our interview questions, we arranged for an article in *The Grand Rapids Press* about religion and abuse, with a sidebar about our project which asked for interview volunteers, not limiting religious affiliation or type of abuse. We received over 200 calls and letters in response, most of which told stories which were diverse yet seemed to have common threads. Many denominations were represented, yet almost all were white Christians. Thus, although we are sensitive to non-Christian religions, we have used the term "church" without including "synagogue" and "Christians" without including other religions.

After listening to the stories, it became clear that the church as a whole has not responded well to cases of abuse, probably because they don't know what to do. This book is written to examine the connections among the church, religious beliefs, and abuse and dispel the idea that abuse "doesn't happen in our church," to be a voice for the stories of survivors who have struggled as a result of their abuse and for whom the church has not always been the haven it should have been, and to inform the church and church members how to respond sensitively, thoughtfully, responsibly, and effectively to the issue of abuse.

This is a book about physical, sexual and/or emotional abuse to people who are or have been members of a church. It is not only about abuse within the family, although much of it falls in that category. It is about the experiences, struggles and reactions of abuse survivors.

vii

Acknowledgements

The authors wish to acknowledge many people who helped this project come about: Ed Golder, then religion editor of *The Grand Rapids Press*, who wrote the initial article recruiting people for us to interview; Calvin College for the alumni grant which allowed us to begin; Beth Goebels and the Dyer-Ives Foundation, which gave us a grant to continue when the project became much bigger than we anticipated; Mel Hugen and Dale Cooper of Calvin College and Charles Honey of *The Grand Rapids Press* for reviewing the manuscript.

We thank the work-study students who tirelessly typed transcripts of interviews.

Most of all, we give thanks to all those survivors who were willing to talk with us. We hope we have treated their stories with the dignity they deserve as we relate them for the reader.

Part I: Background

Chapter 1

No Safe Place

[I told] my mother. She didn't feel that it was that big of a deal. I told her when I was around five. I didn't know that it was bad then. She didn't feel it was that big of a deal so she didn't do anything about it. [Even today I'm] very careful. It's not acceptable still. Even seeing somebody, a psychologist or something, is still not all that acceptable. It's strange how many of us are out there. (Nicole)

Background Information

Abuse is not confined to any one group of people, nor is religion or the church immune. Abuse is not a new phenomenon. The Bible reveals at least three cases of rape. (All Biblical citations in this book are taken from the New International Version (NIV) or the King James Version (KJV)). In two of these cases the victim was avenged by members of her family, however.

In Genesis 34 is found the story of Dinah, daughter of Leah and Jacob. "When Shechem, son of Hamor the Hivite, a ruler of that area, saw her, he took her, and violated her" (verse 2, NIV). Jacob's sons were deeply distressed. However, Shechem realized he loved Dinah, so Hamor asked for Dinah as a wife for his son. Jacob's sons, planning revenge, agreed and asked for a dowry only that all the men become circumcised. "Three days later, while all of them were still in pain," the story reads, two of Jacob's sons killed all the men, took everything they had, and rescued Dinah. The brothers had thus avenged their sister because she had been defiled and disgraced.

Second Samuel 13 tells of the rape of Tamar, daughter of King David, by Amnon, her half-brother. By pretending to be ill and asking for Tamar to come fix his food and feed him, Amnon cunningly set the scene. He did not love his sister, only lusted for her, and quickly raped his prey. Predictably, his lust then turned to hatred and he made her leave. Tamar marked her head with ashes and tore the sleeves from her robe, which indicated she was no longer a virgin daughter of the king. She confided in her other brother, Absalom, who told her to be quiet for now and not think about it, but he hated Amnon for his actions and two years later commanded the servants to kill Amnon when he was "in high spirits from drinking." (NIV)

A third story in Judges 19 of the rape of the concubine[1], however, shows two men's low image of women when one offers his daughter and another gives his concubine to a mob of angry men instead of her master the Levite, the one for whom they shouted. The concubine had left the Levite and spent four months in her father's home in Bethlehem in Judah before he came to bring her back. On the trip back to Ephraim, they stopped in Gibeah for the night. An old man took them in and there was merriment and drinking. A mob pounded on the door wanting the master to rape. The old man protected his guest by offering his virgin daughter and the concubine instead of a man to ravish. When the offer was rejected, the Levite threw his concubine out the door to the men, to protect himself. The mob ravaged and tortured the concubine until morning. "The Greek Bible says, 'for she was dead'...The Hebrew text, on the other hand, is silent, allowing the interpretation that this abused woman is yet alive."[2] Whatever the case, her master took her home, cut her into 12 pieces and "sent her into all the areas of Israel" (19:29, NIV) to show everyone what had been done to him (or his property). He denied any part in the act.

Clearly abuse is evident as a personal trouble in the Bible, but has it become a public issue?

We see that abuse of weak, helpless human beings has always existed, but since Biblical times society has looked the other way, often saying it was a family problem or that such instances were rare. As late as 1824 in Mississippi and 1867 in California, appellate courts upheld the so-called "rule of thumb," which allowed a man to beat his "errant wife" provided the stick he used was no thicker than his thumb. The first case of child abuse in the United States courts was actually prosecuted under the cruelty to animals laws, for there were no others which could be used.

Child abuse finally began to be recognized as a social problem with the publication of a 1962 article on battered child syndrome – physical injuries which could be seen and diagnosed by physicians[3]. By 1967, all states had passed laws making reports of child abuse mandatory, and by 1974 the federal government had established a center for the identification and prevention of child abuse.

Child sexual abuse was seldom noticed even by clinicians prior to 1975, the year the Family Violence Research Program at the University of New Hampshire conducted the first national study on family violence. In subsequent years, recognition of child sexual abuse has spread faster than any other form of child neglect or abuse.

By the 1970s, the women's movement clamored for the rights and protection of women, demanding battered women's shelters, rape crisis centers and research on wife beating. The prevalence of spouse abuse was recognized, and elder abuse was correctly predicted to be the next area addressed. Critical factors cited were longer life expectancy and therefore the increase in the number of older persons, many of whom are dependent on and battered by their adult caretaker children.

It was not until the 1970s that sociologists began a determined study of various forms of abuse. Until that time most scholarly literature on this subject was written by physicians and psychologists, creating an image of abuse as a psychological problem and social factors as essentially irrelevant. A review of research[4] which contributed to the emergence of family violence as a social problem showed that, while part of the goal of research on family violence has been to explode the myth that violence in the home is rare, it also has been to convince people that abuse is extensive enough to be labeled a social problem so funds and energies will be spent on helping those involved.

In 1974, Straus[5] gave two reasons for the emergence of family violence as a sociological issue: the women's movement and the sensitization to violence due to political assassinations, violent social protest, and the Vietnam war. Star[6] went on to identify three factors surrounding the matter of family violence, factors which probably apply to any type of abuse: a) lack of awareness, b) general acceptance, and c) denial.

We must also look at the issue of male dominance of power in the church and family unit as well as the level of stress in the family as contributing elements. One must be careful, however, not to dismiss the fact of husband abuse as well.

In 1983, the International Conference on Psychological Abuse of Children and Youth produced a generic definition of child abuse, with clarification of terms. Four years later, however, psychologists claimed that "little effort has been devoted to research and intervention focused on psychological maltreatment [child abuse and neglect] primarily because available definitions and standards for determining its existence and impact are inadequate."[7]

Turbett and O'Toole[8] found that physicians were more likely to label minority children and those from lower-class families as abused than those from middle- or upper-class white families. Family violence in general is less likely to be *discovered* in middle- and upper-class families. They live in bigger homes which are farther apart than the apartments of the poor, powerless and defenseless. Public clinics and emergency rooms are more likely to suspect and report abuse than are private physicians. Some respondents to a 1990 survey of the prevalence of abuse in the Christian Reformed Church[9] returned blank questionnaires with a notation on the front stating that they were good Christian people and abuse didn't happen in *their* church; the study *did* show, however, that more than one in four (28%) members of the Christian Reformed Church had been abused sexually, physically and/or emotionally. The O. J. Simpson murder trial in 1995 brought into the media tales of spousal abuse by the rich and famous. In fact, abuse happens across all age lines, all socio-economic statuses, all categories of people.

Since the early 1990s, the media has reported the concept of false memories or false memory syndrome (FMS). Some FMS proponents believe that if you didn't always remember something, it never happened. Elizabeth Loftus, a survivor herself and long a researcher into memory, has stated that delayed memories of childhood trauma are falsehoods induced by the suggestions of self-help literature, especially the book *Courage to Heal*[10], and naive or unscrupulous psychotherapists. Loftus' work contributed to the formation of the False Memory Syndrome Foundation, which works to aid those who say they have been falsely accused. Goodman et al.[11] tell us "The research on PTSD [Post Traumatic Stress Disorder] indicates that some children, particularly children who suffer extended traumatic events, may be prone to denial as a defense mechanism" (p. 8). Harvey and Herman[12] state, "Indeed, there is no empirical evidence to suggest that psychotherapy is a factor at all in the *majority* [our emphasis] of cases of delayed recall" (p. 30). In the early 1990s, the American Psychological Association issued some interim conclusions to their investigation of memories of childhood abuse, among which were "it is possible for memories of abuse that have been forgotten for a long time to be remembered. The mechanism, or mechanisms, by which such delayed recall occurs is not currently well understood. It is also possible to construct convincing pseudomemories for events that have never occurred."[13]

According to Myers[14], both those committed to protecting abused children and those committed to protecting wrongly accused adults agree on the following:

- Incest happens.
- Forgetting happens.
- Recovered memories are commonplace.
- Memories "recovered" under hypnosis or the influence of drugs are especially unreliable.
- Memories of things happening before age 3 are also unreliable.
- Memories, whether real or false, can be emotionally upsetting. If a false memory of abuse becomes a real part of one's history, the client as well as the family may suffer. Like real traumas, such experiences can then cause lasting suffering.

In *our* study, 24 of the 61 survivors interviewed had always remembered their abuse, but 37 had at least some delayed recall; memories usually began returning in the form of nightmares, when an offspring reached the age at which they themselves were abused, or when they went into therapy for severe depression knowing something was wrong.

While abuse already has become a *public* issue, it is now emerging as an issue within the church. Denominations are having to wrestle with the problem because accusations about abuse within the church are being publicly disclosed. It is to help the church overcome denial and understand the consequences of abuse that we write this book.

Method

As we began our research, callers responding to the newspaper article described in the Prologue were screened to be certain they fit the religious aspect of our study. We also asked about their healing process and if they would come to the college for an interview. We selected 63 survivors from those who had called to interview (in addition to the five we interviewed as resource people earlier). Criteria for this selection included how far along they were in the healing process, whether they had sought help in dealing with the problems created by their abuse, diversity of religious affiliation, and how well we felt the caller could express him- or herself. As we had calls from very few males, we first selected as many of them as we felt appropriate to our goals, then selected the rest from the females. This resulted in the selection of 9 men and 54 women for interview. One woman canceled her interview at the last moment, having decided she was not ready to talk about her experiences with us. We also conducted one group interview of four volunteers from a support group. We audiotaped each interview and later typed the transcripts.

Preliminary work and interviews with resource persons were conducted during August 1992. Individual and group interviews were done during September, October, and early November 1992. The five basic topics covered were: 1) Background information about the survivor including age and religious affiliation at time of abuse and now. 2) Tell us your story of abuse and where you are in your healing, if that is part of your story. 3) Describe your family when you were abused. What about authority, control, and equality? What was the relationship between spouses? If it was child abuse, what role did the non-offending parent play in abuse, in its enactment, disclosure, treatment, and healing? What is that family like today? 4) Was religion used to justify the abuse? Was religion a help or hindrance to your surviving abuse? Have your religious beliefs and faith been affected by your experience with abuse? How? 5) When you were abused, was your family involved in church? What denomination? Was church involved in any way with your abuse? Did you leave or consider leaving your church because of the abuse? Did you seek out or join another church? How do you feel about church today? About God? Has church in any way been a source of healing for you? How could a church minister better to survivors of abuse? How about to abusers? Describe your ideal church.

Before writing this book, we sent our interviewed survivors a copy of their interview transcript for approval. We wanted to be sure we had permission to use the recorded information from the interviews and to give them the opportunity to delete any information which might make them feel uneasy or identifiable. As some of the tapes had spots where our equipment did not record well, we also wanted to be certain that we had understood correctly what each had said. We have included material only from those interviewees who responded with permission. Unless otherwise requested by them,we have changed all names.

The Survivors

As a group, who were our interviewees? There were 9 males (14.5%) and 53 females (85.5%). At the time of the interview, ages ranged from 19 to 64 years of age, with 83.1% falling in the 30-49 range. When asked their current marital status, 60.0% responded they were in their first marriage; another 26.1% had been married and were either separated, divorced, or remarried. Most had at least some college (83.1%). They attended Sunday morning worship services at least 2-3 times a month (58.4%). As stated earlier, all cases had ties to Christian churches, but there was diversity in those.

Although we did not look at which specific church affiliations changed, we know that 38% of survivors were, at the time of their interview, still in the same denomination as their abusive times; 30%, however, had changed affiliation, and 26% had moved away from the church entirely. (Three percent were unchurched at the time of the abuse and had not become churched at the time of the survey. This does not mean they didn't attend church, only that they did not see themselves as *affiliated* with a denomination.)

Disclaimer

While our study's intent from the start was to serve as a voice for victims of abuse, we recognize that such a study has obvious weaknesses. For example, such a study leaves many questions unanswered. In-depth interview research such as ours cannot provide quantitative data on the prevalence of abuse in society. Our previous survey was successful in estimating the prevalence of abuse within a particular denomination[15] and showed that over one in four (28%) members of the Christian Reformed Church had been physically, sexually and/or emotionally abused. It was our recognition of the weaknesses of that type of study–for example, its inability to let the individual and personal voices of the abused be heard–that prompted this personal interview project. Nevertheless, we want it perfectly clear that, given the methodology of the present study, we can't be certain that our interviewees are representative of the larger population in the nation or even the Grand Rapids area. We are confident, however, that the problems reported by our survivors are widespread and that it is vitally important for the church to hear their voices. Furthermore, we have made no effort to verify the stories shared with us. To do so, we think, would have negatively affected the confidence relationship established with our subjects. Instead, we have taken their stories at face value, for they were perceived as reality to the people we interviewed.

What Follows

In the remainder of this book, we will use survivor answers to five of the research questions to help the reader learn from those who know all too vividly the realities of abuse. Chapter 2, "In the Name of God," examines how religion was used to justify abuse. It will look at Bible verses as well as religious practices and theological beliefs which were used to convince the victim that he or she deserved what was happening.

Chapter 3, "When Churches Deny, Victimization Escalates" examines the responses of the church, both negative and positive. Survivors gave a great many examples of response from not only individuals within the church but also the church as an organization.

Abuse affects its victims in many ways. Chapter 4, "They Pay, You Pay, We All Pay," looks at how those effects expand into many phases of a person's being: fears and anxieties, self and self-esteem, church as an unsure foundation, changes and constraints in behavior, and strained and broken relationships.

"Why, God?", Chapter 5, investigates the abused's attitudes toward religion and church. Why did many leave their church? How do they perceive God, who didn't remove them from the horrors of their experiences? Was the church a help or hinderance in their healing process? What is their current church involvement?

We hope churches will learn from the voices of the survivors. In "Supportive Ventures," the sixth chapter details suggestions from survivors for how the church could help both them and their abusers. And you will learn what the survivors responded when we asked them to describe what they would look for if they thought they could find their "ideal church."

"In Other Words...", the seventh chapter, gives a summary and our recommendations for actions, and lists some resources.

Appendix A is a brief description of each survivor quoted herein. Appendix B contains the interview schedule, those questions we asked each interviewee.

Part II: Survivors Speak Out

Chapter 2

In the Name of God: How Religion Was Used to Justify Abuse

Religion told me that I was bad, and therefore needed to be whipped and chaffed and deserved punishment. If God did everything for my good, how could I be so foolish to go against my own good? So I needed to allow the abuse to happen. Because I had to obey my parents, I needed to stop thinking for myself, and allow my parents to do abusive things that taught me to devalue myself. So religion made me feel powerless. I had to obey my parents no matter what they did because the Bible said to obey and honor your parents. (Bonnie)

I just said, "Is this really O.K.?" I asked him right to his face. I said, "Does God say that this is O.K.?" And he said, "Yeah, God says this is O.K." (Elizabeth)

When we first decided to work on this project, we wanted to look at the connection between religion and abuse – in particular, if and how religion was used to justify abuse. This chapter focuses upon survivor responses to that question.

Responses fell into two main categories. The first was Bible references or verses, and included references to submission, honor or obey, spare the rod and spoil the child, and some unspecified ones like references to being worms. The second main category had to do with religious practices or theological beliefs and included references to the church itself, satanic cults, the roles of men and women as taught by the church, punishment from God, authority from God, references to the devil, abuse in "good Christian families," and pastoral abuse; we also make mention of the abuser's relationship to the church when it was specifically stated. In addition, sometimes the "justification" was used by the abusers themselves and other times was the response of non-abusers in denial that these things could happen. As you read the text, think of the effects each of these behaviors or teachings could have on a person being abused.

Bible Verses/References

While in some cases specific Bible verses were used to justify the abuse, in all cases religion was used in an emotionally abusive way, helping to create or continue the atmosphere under which abuse could persist. Although a few interviewees mentioned specific Bible verses, others referred to verses without mentioning them specifically.

Submission

One of the prevalent threads was the idea of submission, which seems common in many of our patriarchal-based churches. The idea held is that the man is head of the house and the woman should do whatever he tells her. Victims of spouse abuse were told that good wives were submissive. Maureen related specific verses:

> The hardest part to take in that fifteen months of being married to him was getting beaten to the tune of 1 Peter 3 [1] and Ephesians 5 [22-24], that if I didn't learn how to submit, he was going to kill me.

(I Peter 3: 1. *Wives, be submissive to your husbands* (NIV); Eph 5: 22-24. *Wives, submit to your husbands, as to the Lord. For the husband is the head of the wife as Christ is the head of the church, his body, of which he is the Savior. Now as the church submits to Christ, so also wives should submit to their husbands in everything.* (NIV)) The last quote then continues, however, (verse 25) *Husbands, love your wives, just as Christ loved the church, and gave himself for her* (NIV). Perhaps the real eye-opener comes in verse 28: *In this same way, husbands ought to love their wives as their own bodies.*

He who loves his wife loves himself (NIV). Often men who abuse do so because they feel incompetent themselves and feel the wife (and perhaps family) is one area where they can show power. These are *not* people who love themselves. Perhaps they *do* treat their wives as they feel about themselves.

Sarah referred to the same idea without being specific. She also recognized an important factor in abuse – control over the victim. Without that control, the abuse could not continue, if it ever got started.

> As we got further into the marriage, he started bringing the Bible into it, and how I should be like the women in the Bible – according to him – submissive. He started underlining Bible quotations and I was supposed to follow these, because that's what the good wife did. It even got down to the point that women should eat dirt. I never even heard that in the Bible...He had a really strange thing about the Bible. I don't know. It was used for his benefit is what I'd say. What he could use to control me was the Bible is what it amounted to. He used it as a control factor.

Honor or Obey

Likewise, interviewees who had been abused as children referred to being told to obey or honor their parents, as in Eph 6: 1-2 (*Children, obey your parents in the Lord, for this is right. Honor your father and mother*)[16] (NIV).

Maggie was told she should obey her parents in whatever they wanted her to do. "We had to obey the church and we had to obey our parents. God will get you if you don't. It was pretty strict."

In the same vein, Jessica related, "My dad would always say, 'Honor thy father and mother' and it was words written in the Bible that I had to do everything they wanted."

Once again, unfortunately, the abuser should have continued reading, for verse 4 goes on to say, "*Fathers, do not provoke your children: but bring them up in the nurture and admonition of the Lord*" (KJV).

One addition to the Biblical verse was thrown at Elizabeth, who was told she would go to Hell if she was bad or didn't obey. "You feel like it was your fault and God holds you responsible for what happened."

For Anne, the threat was even deeper. Her parents were not content to refer to Ephesians 1-2, but added verse 3 as well (*That it may go well with you, and you may enjoy long life on the earth*) (NIV). In other words, if she didn't honor her parents, which she just couldn't do given the extensive abuse, she would *not* live long...she would die, and die young.

Christy learned that "we should respect and obey our parents, which usually meant both of them, but men had the dominance" and she was supposed to do whatever they told her to. This teenager showed some insight, however, when she talked about the impact of that teaching on her being abused:

> They told you what to do. And you should do it without question. And that's probably why I was quiet for so long.

Spare the Rod and Spoil the Child

Nicole's physical abuse was justified by yet another quote, "Spare the rod and spoil the child," as her parents told her it was their duty to punish her. Although oft used, this is not a quote per se from the Bible. Closest references are Proverbs 22:15 (*Foolishness is bound in the heart of a child; but the rod of discipline will drive it far from him.*) or chapter 23: 13-14 (*Withhold not discipline from the child: for if you beatest him with the rod, he shall not die. Thou shalt beat him with the rod, and shalt deliver his soul from hell*) (KJV).

Bonnie was also among those threatened with this so-called quote.
> The Christian family is to obey parents. If I didn't obey my parents, the Bible said they needed to beat me in order to not spoil me. Like 'spare the rod and spoil the child' type of thing.

Unspecified

Abuse victims usually have low self-esteem, which enables the abuser to manipulate them. It may be existing or developed by the perpetrator(s). Although Ryan was unaware of the Bible as a source, it was used to ensure low self-esteem so he would feel unworthy and undeserving of help:

> My dad put a lot of emphasis on us kids being worms, under some song in the hymnal, and I don't even know where it came from, but something like 'such a worm as I.' He really hammered that in, to be humble and meek and to be a worm,

not to think much of yourself.

One reference to the worm is found in the NIV in Ps 22:6 *But I am a worm and not a man; scorned of men and despised by the people. And Job 25:4, 6: How then can a man be righteous before God? How can one born of a woman be pure? ... How much less man, who is a but a maggot? and the son of man, who is only a worm?*

Without citing verses, Maureen talked of the Bible's treatment of women as a justification for abusers: "There's a lot of places in the Old Testament where I can read into it that women are treated like a piece of property."

And although Charlene didn't have Biblical verses used by her abuser, a Sunday School teacher put fear of the devil into her when as a child she tried to tell what was happening to her (Charlene suffers from Dissociative Identity Disorder or multiple personalities as a result of her abuse):

> I told somebody at church; one of us in here told one of my mother's friends and she was a lady I liked, I think she was a Sunday school teacher, maybe mine, and one of us told her that bad things were happening to us. She said, "Don't ever say anything like that about your father, you'll go to the lake of fire." So we didn't tell anybody anymore. 'Cause we already knew a lot about lakes of fires and things.

(Rev. 20: 10 *And the devil that deceived them was cast into the lake of fire and brimstone, where the beast and the false prophet are, and shall be tormented day and night for ever and ever*) (KJV).

Religious Practices/Theological Beliefs

Several themes of religious practices or theological beliefs emerged: the church itself, satanic cults, rules of men and women as taught by the church, punishment from God, mandate from God, references to the devil, abuse in "good Christian families," and pastoral abuse. We see some of the many ways abusers use theology to aid in their crimes.

Church

Maggie's father let the church and its rules set up his victims. Her mother was very religious and took the children to services every Sunday. She related:

My father didn't go to church, and so it isn't the typical case where he's got the Bible in his hand. It's very, very subtle, though, and very, very clever. First of all, we went to church with my mom, and we believed everything they told us in church. And then my dad demeaned her and made fun of the Pope. And that just made us crazy. He always looked wiser, so then she always looked like a ditz that she would believe that stuff, especially as I got to be a teen. But what he did was, he allowed the church to tear down our self-esteem and he allowed the church to get us to be passive. So he allowed the church to do all his ground work for him. And then he could come in and abuse us.

Churches must stop and look at how some of their teachings can affect people who are in abusive situations. Sunday Schools can teach doctrine, but also must emphasize the worth and self-esteem of their students; when they don't, there can be tragic results. For Brianna, the church itself, or at least its teaching and preaching, added to her abuse and feelings of powerlessness.

I think, in the particular church that I was raised in, there's such an emphasis on being sinners and bad. It was so hard to sit there and listen to that and just praying a silent prayer and praying, "God, I'm a good girl. Please just make this stop." I really got the impression that God was a very wrathful, angry God, and that we could never be good enough anyway.

Heather had somewhat the same experience, with church teachings adding to her guilt and frustrations.

But it was the way church was viewed from the home – it was the ultimate authority. And the church would frown on you because you were always sinful. We carried these little biblical phrases that said you could never do anything good in the eyes of God, and that sort of thing, to the point where nothing you could do would be good...My mother always prayed for the sins of omission. I always had a feeling that I was doing something wrong, and I didn't know what it was...my mother prayed in a vein that was always aimed at everybody else. But you have to remember, my mother had no sins, so I mean, it was very pointless to pray for yourself. Anything she did that you might construe as being wrong, was done because either we made her nervous, or we had sinned first. Or if she lost her temper it was because we had done something wrong.

Christy saw her father's interpretation of the teachings of the Mormon church as support for his abusive behavior.

They can have as many wives as they want, while I guess in my father's eyes, as many wives as he wants would be like taking his daughters and counting them as wives.

Satanic Cults

Some interviewees talked of being taken to the "Satanic church" by their abusers. Listening to the experiences that our survivors of satanic abuse endured, we realized how serious a situation this is. The problem is enhanced by the many people who deny that the cults exist, thus denying these survivors' victimizations.

Many victims of Satanic cults developed multiple personalities or Dissociative Identity Disorder (DID) to deal with the horrors they endured. Charlene spoke of moving around and her father seeking out a cult or satanic church wherever they moved.

And then we found one, and this was a huge house, only this house had pornography, too, as part of it. It was a huge mansion, and they had one area where they did experiments and then they had another area where they did this pornography stuff. And there was a lady that lived there and she was really fat and she liked to do sexual things to the children, too. And there was another area where they did the rituals and the sacrifices and things like that and in that one, one time we had to write our names in Satan's book and then get raped by Satan, or whoever it was. And there was a lady there that was really old and she was very cold. Her hands were cold and she knew just how to hurt you, to make you do what she wanted you to do. I think we went there on Sunday afternoon after church.

Charlene told us that her parents were seen by the Christian church as "good Christians," but after church they all went to the Satanic cult! Later, she spoke specifically of one of the atrocities she endured. This is included here to help the reader understand some of the terrible things people do to others. (Remember, Charlene was a victim of D.I.D., thus the use of the word "we".)

One time when we were seven, we found a baby baking in the oven and we weren't suppose to look, but we did. And he was one year old, I think, something like that and they were going to eat him that night at a feast; and because we saw that, then they chained us up because we weren't suppose to see it and they would not let us go until we agreed to help them kill the mother of the baby. Because they were a mother and a baby that didn't have family and this lady did not have husband or anything. So they took her in, you know, to be nice to her. Through the time that we were in that cult, there were a lot of people like that. They took in people that did not have homes. So they let us go, off of the chains and they gave us this dagger and somebody else put his hand around our hand and just chomped it in. And a lot of different kinds of things like that happened.

Lacey had many of the same types of Satanic experiences, and talked of being dedicated by her parents to Satan.

I was married to Satan when I was nine. When I was 15 my dad did a ceremony to make me Mary, the mother of Jesus, and at 18 I was dedicated to the devil...I'm not sure when I was branded, but I am branded here to Satan.

Roles of Women and Men

We asked what our survivors had learned in church about women and about men. These responses point up that they were taught submissiveness for women and children and the powerfulness of men, characteristics which can support the abusive tendencies of some. Maggie talked about women as being selfless people who should give all to their husbands:

I learned we were supposed to be good. If we would just give to our husband or our children, that would give us contentment and serenity. We should not have a need or a thought of our own. And society said that, too. And my dad said that, too.

Several others also talked about religious teachings which served to justify abuse, including the roles of women and men. Ryan learned much the same as Maggie, again reinforcing the "submissive" theme.

I learned that women were second-class citizens, that they did not have as much power. Growing up in the Christian Reformed Church, women were secondary. When they had a consistory meeting there was only one vote per family, and it was the man that voted. My dad really reinforced that, too. Women weren't supposed to do this in the church and weren't supposed to do that; women were supposed to just show up and have the ladies aid society. The women were

supposed to be submissive; that's what I've learned in the church.
Kim was a little more succinct:

You were controlled by the man in the family and you didn't have a
say in anything. You were to submit to whatever was asked of you.

As much of the Bible is written according to the times of the writer,
many stories and narratives tend to demean women. Maureen saw the
church using Old Testament ideas to dilute the personhood of women.

Christianity gave us personhood. And with that personhood there
were still a lot of views, those Old Testament, old time views, that
women were property. "Don't talk in church. Wear your hat." Those
literal things that kept the culture from twisting and staying into
view. "Women keep quiet." Well, if they said anything, would
anyone listen to them?

Charlene was asked if her non-offending mother was docile because
that's what she thought the church wanted. She replied, "Partly. She
believes that women are supposed to be in submission and obedience
to their husbands and my father believed that, too."
Michael's education added children to the category of women,
which is important to consider in the justification of child abuse, as
many victims are male. Once again, the rules set the child up for
abuse.

The religious aspect was very much that you had your role. The
women were subservient. Children kept their mouths shut. You
know, there's probably about five billion rules for a good Christian
boy, and I learned them young. When you were around adults, you
kept your mouth shut. You never talked back to adults. You never
talked back to your teachers. They were always right.

On the other hand, many religions teach a superiority and
powerfulness about men. Michael's learning supported that idea of
headship as taught in some religions:

The father runs the family. That's what we heard in church. That's
what was preached. That's what we were taught in school, the male's
role. And in our family – my family – my father was and is extremely
religious in terms of being involved with church and church
activities and everything else. The men were dominant.

Ryan also learned it. He said that men "had more power, it was a whole lot better being a man than it was being a woman. [Men] were the first class citizens. " Men were the head of the house. Kim learned that men "were like God. They never did any wrong, anything wrong. And you always obeyed them, especially if it was your father or your husband."

Maggie responded to the question in much the same way.

> I learned that men were smart. They were intelligent. They were strong. They made the best decisions. We should follow them. Plus the church is the family picture and the man had the power. Whether it be the Pope or the Father, they had the power and the women were irrelevant. And my family structure is like that. My dad had all the power and my mom had none.

But then she added a zinger which created guilt for her and guarded against her telling:

> The church kind of taught us that men would be sexual and they couldn't help it. But women shouldn't be. There were two kinds of women. The good kind and then the bad girls. But men had these sexual drives and they couldn't help that. It's our job to control that. I think society tells us that, too.

Punishment from God

Another theme was that of God's punishment. Several victims were kept subservient with threats, making them feel their abuse was justified, that their actions had caused it. They were taught that God is harsh and vindictive, not loving and forgiving. Michael related that religion was not used to justify the abuse per se:

> Nothing like, well "God says I may rape you" or whatever. It was very much the way, "if you tell anybody you will be punished." I do remember him saying things like, "God will punish you, you've been a very naughty boy." My abuser was an elder in the church until he was about 50. You know, the elder says it's true, that's it. There's no argument. What any adult says is the way it is. And, truthfully, if you're naughty, God's going to get you, and basically, the strict background is what I was raised on. And I remember him telling me what a naughty boy I'd been, I'd just been a terribly naughty boy, and that I had to be punished. And I kept saying "No, I haven't. I haven't done anything." "Yeah, you've been naughty. Don't you

learn anything in Sunday school?" When I was spanked as a kid it
wasn't because Mom and Dad wanted to, it was because I was
naughty and God said I had to be punished.

Maggie was also taught about a God of vindictiveness instead of
love. "God was always someone who was going to get you. And you
never could be good enough." Similarly, Kayla's father talked about
"his God he had that would get us all for being bad. He used to tell us
that we were totally depraved. We would never amount to anything."
Jessica learned much the same. The following interchange took
place with the interviewer, whose comments are in italics, after she said
that an aunt referred to her as the devil's child:

*Did you feel perhaps that God thought you were the devil's child,
too?*

Yes, I was so afraid of God, so afraid of Him.

What made you afraid of God?

He was going to strike me dead, especially if I didn't listen to my
parents.

*You thought being dead would be worse than what you were going
through?*

If you went to hell, yes...

Ryan took somewhat the opposite view. He saw a God who didn't
think much of him because he was a "worm," but not a punishing
God; he saw one who readily forgave – perhaps too readily. When
asked if religion was used to justify his abuse, he responded:

In a way; it was always that we were all sinners and if we asked for
forgiveness then we were forgiven. I got the impression that we
could go out and do anything we wanted as long as we acted
sorrowful, knocked ourselves down, acted like a worm, repented,
then we were saved. Then it was okay. So, yeah, in that way it was
justified. My dad could go out and do whatever he wanted, and all
he had to do is say he's sorry and then it is okay.

Authority from God

Along the same line were those survivors who related their abusing
father told them he was the same as or right next to God and therefore
to be obeyed. Emily talked about her father:

> I was taught that dad and God were the same thing. They were so
> intertwined they could not be separated. It was like God is number
> one, God is perfect. Then comes dad, then mom, then older brothers,
> and then...It was like a mandate from God for my father to control his
> children, to be authoritarian over them. We attended church twice
> every Sunday. I know that's not necessarily religion, but we did
> attend church. We were taught to sit still in church and my dad kept
> a straight pin on the lapel of his jacket and if we misbehaved he
> would poke us with the straight pin. And we dared not move.
> Another thing he did to us in church was bend our fingers like this
> and squeeze them, and we could not flinch or we would be taken out
> and he would spank us.

For Lacey, the brainwashing was that Daddy and Jesus were the
same. How could she rebel against Jesus?

> When I was three and I first started going to Sunday school my
> mother told us that Daddy and Jesus are the same. Daddy is just as
> old as Jesus was when he started his ministry and stuff like that.
> Jesus and Daddy are the same and that really confused me, and in the
> three-year-old brain, Jesus and Daddy, Jesus and Daddy, they're the
> same. I have got memories of my dad saying "Jesus said, 'Come unto
> me. I love you.'" And then he would have sex with me.

Lydia related growing up in a similar situation. Her father was
"next to God," she was told, and would inform Him about all her
misbehaving, if she didn't do what dad wanted.

> Growing up I thought that I was a bad person with my dad always
> emphasizing how bad we were; and he would threaten us not only
> physically, he was next to God. God, the minister, our principal,
> and then my dad – so he had the power, he had more of an inside line
> to God than what we did so we weren't going to have a good word
> in because my father would tell Him how bad we were.

Bonnie's parents also expressed a mandate from God to justify her
abuse, even if obeying her father meant not worshipping in church on
Sundays.

Religion and authority is like God gave my parents authority, and who was I to question God?...And if I didn't follow God's command to obey them, I deserved being locked up in a closet, or put in a cedar chest, or being sexually abused or beaten. That type of thing seemed to be a common thing that I felt when I was growing up. At one point in time, it was like going to religious meetings on Sunday afternoons. It was like Sunday was God-ordained. Sunday is for families. But that also meant that I couldn't go and enrich my spiritual life, but I had to stay home for my father to abuse me on Sunday. It was almost like a religious ritual.

Young children tend to say what they are thinking, and Elizabeth was no different from others. Even though she was only five when the sexual abuse began, she was blunt about it with her abuser.

I asked him right out – it just seemed wrong because you had to sneak and you had to be quiet or whatever, and "nobody can know that this happened" and "don't ever tell anybody." I just said, "Is this really O.K.?" I asked him right to his face. I said, "Does God say that this is O.K.?" And he said, "Yeah, God says this is O.K."

Nicole's father used a not-uncommon justification among pedophiles. He told her he had a mandate from God, but it was somewhat different. "I remember my dad telling me that this was his duty to God, to teach me about sex..."

When children are taught that God is perfect and all powerful, and that their abusers are the same as God, it is not surprising that those children may become afraid not only of the abuser but of God as well. They think that if the abuser treats them this way, an all-powerful God will be even harsher.

References to the Devil

In several cases, the devil was used to keep victims in line. One example was mentioned earlier when Charlene was threatened with going to the lake of fire if she ever told anyone else. In addition, she related trying to tell her mother what her father was doing to her:

And at one time one of us, one of us in here tried to tell our mother what was going on and she got real angry and she was ironing when we told her, and she took off the clothes we had on and she put us on the ironing board and she was going to iron us on the back. And she was screaming for Satan to get out and the demons to leave. And then after that she didn't want to take care of anybody any more. She didn't want to take care of us. She didn't want to feed us or anything, and she wouldn't look at us or touch us.

References to the devil were used to keep Jessica feeling worthless. She was told over and over that she was evil, the "devil's daughter."

My family always told my brother and me that we were the evil wicked ones, and my grandmother told me that I was the devil's daughter and she also told me that when I looked into the mirror that it was the devil looking back at me. My aunt would always tell me I wasn't going to go to heaven anyway because I wasn't one of the chosen ones. I was the devil's daughter. She was going to heaven, my parents were going to heaven, my grandparents...I got to a point and I thought if they're all going to be in heaven, why do I want to be there with them?

Anita's mother accused her of being filled with the devil when she refused to accept a doctor's admonition that she would never walk again because of a birth defect.

My mother was very rigid in her thinking, very much bent on "hell thinking." And she said, "You know, you're just like my sister that died in my arms. She was stubborn; you're stubborn just like her, that's why she committed suicide. And she is in hell right now today, and if you don't shape up, if you won't start doing what this doctor says and doing what we tell you to do, stop walking and get back in that wheel chair and get those braces on, you are going to go to hell! That's where you're going to land. If you don't, you do not belong to the Lord." And that was drilled in me all the days of my life, because she saw my fight to walk as being so rebellious.

Abuse in "Good Christian families"

The idea that abuse doesn't happen in "good Christian families" was dispelled by many. Some talked of the double lives their families lived, looking like the perfect family to the outside while abuse occurred within the home. Often the abusers were very active in the church. Interviewees spoke of being abused all during the week and being forced to appear as the perfect family in church on Sunday. From the following examples, one can see how the abuser could fool others and confuse the victim.

Ryan briefly mentions this Jekyll and Hyde behavior. "My dad showed real well. The way my dad was outside the home is tons different than how my dad was inside of the home."

For Michael it was much the same. (Grandpa was his abuser.)

> Our family is very involved in religious activities. Grandpa went to church twice every Sunday, he never missed. I don't think I missed church twice on Sunday until I was probably in my teenage years. You know, we went come hell or high waters, snow, rain, sleet, whatever, we went. The act of religion was very much there. We read the Bible after every meal. We prayed before and after every meal. Our meals were very set. At Grandpa's house it was the same thing – always done that way.

And Jessica described her abusing parents and grandparents, who would swear and holler at each other in the home, but:

> ...if they were out in public it was like they probably have the best marriage in the entire world and they were always very polite and there was the life that they showed to the world and when we got behind the doors of the house it was totally different.

Charlene described her family situation in more detail:

> [My parents] went to church a lot. Their backgrounds were very fundamentalist. So they believed in praying for salvation, in the second birth and all that kind of thing. We went to church in the morning, and we went to church at night on Sunday, and usually we went to church on Wednesday. My father sometimes did the preaching when the minister was away. My mother, since I was four years old, taught Bible clubs every week in her home. So we were almost like a model family, that's the way people thought of us. But then there was this dark side to our family. And, although I can't say for sure, I think I was dedicated as an infant to the satanic cult. It's so strange you know on the one side to be dedicated in a Christian church and then on the other side to be dedicated to a satanic cult.

She went on to describe one portion of that dark side of her "religious" family, telling that "My father used to pray with my sister and me and abuse us under the covers together while he was praying with us."

Church attendance seems to have been important in many of the cases we discussed. It was also important in Kayla's family, and they put on the proverbial good face each week.

We would have to go to church, and it didn't matter what was happening. It didn't matter how bad the chaos was, but we had to pack up and dress up and act like life was wonderful and go and sit in church, and it didn't make much sense to me.

As can be seen, just because a person is active in church or church activities doesn't mean he or she is a "good Christian." Too many people readily conclude that regular church-going makes a good Christian, which isn't necessarily true if you have something to hide; then it makes a good cover-up.

Pastoral Abuse

Another aspect of abuse by "good Christians" happens when the betrayal is by church officials themselves, for example, someone in a pastoral position who should be compassionate and caring to all of his or her parishioners. A surprising number of the cases in this study had suffered this abuse, both male and female. Consider Maggie's pain: "I was sexually abused by the priest...He couldn't be wrong, he was the priest." And Jessica's matter-of-factness: "The minister that was at our church when I was growing up also abused me, as did the janitor." Beatrice was abused by her dad first, then her brother, then when she was eight or nine by a family friend who was a minister. The minister made certain of her silence by telling her that no one would believe the minister would do anything wrong. Then she told of how being abused by a minister affected her. This person who is supposed to epitomize trust and reflecting God had destroyed her.

I would sleep over at my friend's house just so that I wouldn't have to go to church, and it wasn't my church, but still it was a minister who I thought was, you know, wonderful. By him doing what he did to me, I didn't feel like I could trust anybody after that. I couldn't trust anyone.

As we said, not only females were abused by their pastor. When Martin talked about it, his sentences became very short and to the point, emphasizing his pain.

The abuser was a priest. It was sexual abuse. We were taught to respect the Church. That's the way my parents thought. That's the way I thought. The priest was a real representative of the Church who shouldn't do things like he was doing.

Not only children were abused. People need to understand that just because a person is an adult doesn't mean he or she has the emotional power to walk away. Melissa was an adult when her pastor sexually abused her. He used his power as a "man of God" to keep the relationship going.

> I always used to think of [the pastor] as the man of God. And the man of God did it, you know? He knew what he wanted. He used sex in such a way that he kept me unbalanced. He would take it to a certain point and then walk out the door. And it would leave me feeling maybe I did something wrong...There are two women, non-church women, whom he approached basically as, "Hi, I'm Dean. I'm with the church and we have a fund for needy people, and I just heard that you lost your job. Could you use some money?" And then the basic thing would be, he'd get into the house. And then, it's, "Well, here's the twenty, twenty-five dollars" – it varied – "I helped you. Now, can you help me?" And he'd get his sexual encounters that way, also. So in a sense he wasn't using God to justify it, but he used his position as a Christian as a means of gaining an entry.

In some cases, the pastor's actions encouraged abuse by the parent. Charlene realized that the minister's conduct taught her father some new tricks:

> I have these really vague memories of being taken to some church, to the minister in the church, and I can see the couch and the lamp and everything. And he was supposed to do something to help me. I don't know why they thought something was wrong with me, but they did. And what he did then, was he took my underwear off and he stuck his fingers inside of me while he prayed. So my dad was doing all this stuff at home.

Only Frank had any type of religious "justification" for not ending the abuse. His abuser had treated him tenderly, in one respect:

> The major abuse in my life was with a preacher. He was one person who seemed truly glad that I existed, happy to see me every time, and that was something I needed very badly at that time. "Why did you keep going back to this situation?" you might ask, and the answer has considerable religious overtones; it seems to me that the answer is that we all seek for a sense of worth that only God can eventually

fill.   And this man gave me indications that I was worthwhile in
ways that I didn't get anywhere else.   That sense of worth was just a
response that I had to his actions, to his being glad that I existed.

But he followed with the frustration of many victims:

> I did not have what it took to reason with him, I guess.   I did not
> have the fortitude to simply stand up and say "You will not do this,
> I don't care what you say."   There were many times when I wanted to
> do that.

Erica suffered severe emotional abuse from her pastor, who slandered
her, then sent elders to her home to tell her and her husband they
would be subject to church discipline for telling lies about the pastor.
Later, when she had a dire medical diagnosis, he refused to visit her.
"I call that emotional abuse because he couldn't separate being a pastor
from personal anger."

In summary, survivors told us that religion *was* used to justify their
abuse.   For some, it was references to specific Bible verses, such as
those about submission or about honoring or obeying their parents.   In
some cases religious practices or theological beliefs were used to
condone abusive situations.   In particular, themes of the church itself,
rules of men and women as taught by the church, punishment from
God, references to the devil, abuse in "good Christian families," and
pastoral abuse appeared in these interviews.

Responses of interviewees have shown us how damaging, under
some circumstances, can be the teachings of the church or the words of
someone in authority who should be trustable.   We must learn how to
respond more helpfully in cases of abuse and how to help victims
escape and grow as beloved children of God.

Chapter 3.

When Churches Deny, Victimization Escalates: Response of the Church

> *My sister told my brother that the priest had intercourse with her and afterward she wasn't feeling right about this. In fact, she didn't feel right about the whole thing, the whole time. "This isn't right." She said, "Father, I've sinned." Father says, "Go to confession, don't worry about it."*
> *...Instead of dealing with the problem, they buried it and hid it. To me that's corruption, they're not thinking of their lambs, us. They don't think of taking care. Instead of saying I'm sorry, he started talking about his life, and his experiences as a priest, how he has never run across this before. That didn't reassure me a whole lot, because I knew what went on; I saw it. I saw the abusive priest; I saw the priest's friend who didn't do anything about the abuse when he suspected something was going on. Or I think he should have suspected.* Martin on the abuse of himself and his sister

Many survivors said or alluded to the fact that people within the church simply do not know how to respond to cases of abuse. How *has* the church responded to situations of abuse? If we believe in a God of love, we expect the church should be a place of comfort, hope, caring, and peace, and its response to hurting people would echo that. But that is only sometimes the case, as shown by many of our survivors.

We examine here the responses of the church as experienced by our survivors. We first look at the negative responses, which included disinterest, rejection, physical violence, denial, unrealistic expectations,

27

lack of patience, and merely moving the offender. There were positive responses, too, which are examined beginning on page 35 and can give the reader some suggestions for helpful response. They include verbal support, physical support, use of trained lay persons, not forcing forgiveness, supportive sermons, counseling funds, and the removal of an offending pastor.

Negative Responses

Not all victims had been able to talk to anyone at church about their pain. For example, Maggie said of the church, "That's not where I would ever take it." Others felt a definite negative reaction of the church to their situations, revictimizing the victim by being judgmental instead of caring.

As will be seen in some of the following sections, Maureen had a wide variety of negative responses from the church. They began *during* her spousal abuse, and she experienced disinterest, rejection, and denial on the part of the church.

Disinterest

Maureen talked about her experiences when her husband was beating and starving her and wouldn't let her attend church.

> Without bothering to come out and find out what was wrong, or caring at all, they tried to remove my membership. Just because I wasn't coming to church. Nobody bothered to find out if there was a problem, or to care, or to feed me. All they cared about was that you walked through those doors on Sunday.

Kayla echoed Maureen's frustration and perhaps gave an explanation for the lack of action from the church when she said, "It was almost like the church didn't want to get involved in what might be going on behind closed doors." These responses emphasize the attitude of some churches that what goes on behind closed doors is "family business," and not the business of others.

Lydia experienced disinterest from her minister when she asked for help about her abuse.

> I told the minister – that was the time that my husband and I were separated – I told him about my abuse. We talked for a little while and he just kind of discounted that fact that I had been sexually

abused and physically abused. He wanted to focus more on what
was happening now. He didn't really want to deal with the abuse;
he wanted to deal with the marital problems.

He discounted the abuse, feeling that if the marital problems were resolved
the abuse would go away. But people must learn that abuse is not the fault
of the victim. It is the *abuser* who has the problems which must be dealt
with for the abuse to stop.

Edna had an experience during her abuse as a child. She related her
reasoning as a child of six and how the priest's disinterest in her
confession led her to the conclusion she was adulterous.

> I told the priest in the confessional that I was sexually abused and I
> think he thought I was a child who didn't understand the Ten
> Commandments, because our church did base a lot of spirituality
> upon the Ten Commandments. And I think that he didn't understand
> or he didn't pursue the subject with me. I told him I was dirty. I told
> him I committed adultery, because, as a child, I related that sexual
> abuse as an adulterous act. That's how I understood it as a child of
> six. And he just never broadened the conversation with me. So I
> just accepted the fact that it was okay, that I told the priest and that
> was what I was supposed to do.

As caring members of God's kingdom, we must pay attention to the
voices of our hurting. We must learn to listen.

Rejection

After Maureen left her abusing husband, she sought out her pastor
who proceeded to revictimize her with rejection instead of responding
with the desired compassion.

> When I did finally get home, I went to go see the pastor to maybe get
> some strength. And I had been abused so bad it took me two months
> before I started to talk, because it didn't matter what I said, I got beat.
> Then I finally started talking a little bit. I went to see the pastor a
> week after I left him. And instead of a hug or caring or reaching out,
> all I heard was, "Don't ever expect to get married in this church
> again." Because then I would be a divorced woman; I was like a mar
> on their record.

She continued to search for help from the church, only to be turned
away over and over again.

I would go to pastors, reaching out, screaming for help. And all they would do was tell me that I was feeling sorry for myself. Or my faith isn't strong enough, or I just needed to pray harder. If I ever did confide to any extent to someone in the church, it went through that church so fast that I became such an outcast. "Oh, that's why she thinks that way." It was impossible to go to things like Coffee Break because my opinions and views of the Bible were drastic because of what I lived through. Well, maybe they are, but maybe you could learn from them, too.

When they were little girls, several of the women had told the priest in confessional of their abuse, using words the priest didn't take time to understand. The lack of support made the girls think what was happening to them was all right. Robin related the circumstances of her rejection, in a situation similar to Edna's earlier quote:

A priest would be [at school] in the daytime and he would hear our confession. And I knew what had happened to me was not right or anything. And I also felt real responsible for that. And I had a little list of the Ten Commandments and all the different ways you could break each one, you know? By process of elimination, I had decided that what had happened was called adultery. And I told the priest that, and he laughed at me. And then right there in front of all my classmates – they were sitting in the pews – he just had a wonderful time with this. It was just so funny he couldn't stand it.

Brianna was both rejected and victimized by the church her abusing husband joined when she filed for divorce.

My husband refused to move out after I filed. He quickly joined a church that adheres to fundamental ideology and began an all-out war against me. He was able to use my sexual abuse history against me within the church and with subsequent "Christian counselors." One woman who claimed to be an expert in incest survivors and was also claiming to be a Christian counselor completely ignored my pain and was enamored with my husband's conversion. She testified against me in court and claimed that my husband should have full custody of my children. This was devastating! My husband was abusive and punitive and absent during the child rearing and now a complete stranger was telling me that I was transferring my anger towards my father to my husband and I should even be hospitalized.

Physical Violence

For one survivor who had been sexually abused by her pastor, some
of the reaction from the church came in the form of physical violence
and intimidation. Melissa talked about the situation:

> He turned the community against me. My car was vandalized; the
> engine blew on my way to seminary one day. If I had been headed
> into work in town, I would have been stranded on the highway. We
> had people driving past the house late in the evening, stop the car,
> slam the car doors, obscenities screamed out at the house. Just any
> intimidation tactic.

Denial

Some people find denial the easiest way to deal with an abuse
disclosure. Michael said, "We use our church to escape responsibility
in a lot of things, and I think they do it with abuse because it's not a
nice subject." One pastor told Maureen:

> Don't even bother to tell me. You have a persecuting spirit...Don't
> spread your views. Keep them to yourself. We don't want to hear
> them. Don't rock our boat. We don't care what you've lived
> through. We don't care to hear about it.

For Latoya, help was there, but it wasn't. Denial was evident in
that the church didn't want anyone to know she was hurting.

> They tried to help in a way but it was like, "We'll help you as long
> as you keep everything under the carpet." And that wasn't much
> help. It seemed like they really didn't *know* how to help. And they
> didn't really want to admit the extent even if the signs were all there
> and stuff, they didn't want to admit that it happened. They didn't
> want to deal with it.

Actions by the church showed Kim their denial. It was another
instance of the attitude that "good Christian people" wouldn't do such
a thing.

> For the most part, the older ones that are from the church are just
> kind of "No, no, no, this doesn't happen." I think so much of how the
> church just really helped destroy me. You know, when they wanted
> to excommunicate me and not preaching anything off the pulpit, I
> mean, it was just a taboo subject; and they never even addressed my

father's drinking problem. It's like, "Oh, he must be under a lot of stress."

Robin finally got up the nerve to disclose, and selected a teacher, a Catholic nun with whom she thought she had been close. But her trust was dashed against the stones by the nun's reaction of denial.

> She was my sixth grade teacher, but I don't think I was in sixth grade anymore. And she was a nun. I thought we were good buddies and I could talk to her. And I told her about it. And then she said that I had no right to make up such incredible lies about my, quote, "fine, upstanding Christian parents." She was calling me a liar. You know, I made the whole thing up; it didn't matter; it didn't count. They were unquestionably fine, upstanding Catholic people. My God, they were sending me to Catholic schools. What else could I want from them?

Although it didn't happen in his case, Michael related an incident he was very familiar with in another church.

> A friend goes to a...church. Their ex-pastor there has raped a number of women in the church and in a couple of other churches, and the denomination has put him out and half that church wants him back as a preacher. In spite of the fact that he has raped at least two women in the church – two girls who are now women. Even the denomination, with the biasedness that the minister's union has for other ministers, put him out. You still get half the people who won't accept it because somehow they can't. If you accept the abuse, you have to admit that you did do something wrong. I know some of the men who are blaming this girl who is sixteen, "She was so sexual. She seduced him."

He then spoke words which many in denial should listen to. They add reality to the whole situation.

> But God knows that's your preacher. Stop and hear what you're saying. This guy had no right under any circumstances, for any reason...I don't care if she stood naked in front of him, he did not have a right to rape her. But somehow that makes it okay because they can somehow accept the fact that – and I suspect they may have known what was going on because some of the things that came out...some people should have known.

As with several other survivors, Anita's church responded with denial, lack of confidentiality, and disinterest. Not only did the council act irresponsibly, the pastor denied what she said and showed an extreme lack of compassion.

And one Christian Reformed church that we went to we had to ask for some help for medication from the deaconate and the church had a lot of doctors in it and they somehow got involved and figured that I was a dope addict and I didn't need to go to a psychiatrist at all. And nobody needed to go through that much on drugs. And so they tried to confront the doctor that I was going to...I also tried to tell a pastor. I want to say that too, that I did try to tell a pastor at one time several years back. I had been married. He felt it was depression that I had been in. But I said I had multiple personalities not depression. And I said, "You know, when I was four and a half years old..." and I told him what happened. I think that I thought then, and I think now, that was the Holy Spirit working in my heart. And this was maybe ten years ago. And he said, "You have to be crazy to think that a kid four and a half years old would feel that." So that kind of turned me off from pastors.

Unrealistic Expectations

Lacey encountered unrealistic expectations on the part of her pastor's wife, who thought she could equate a "quick fix." Her intentions were good, she just wasn't prepared for what she got into.

Mental, emotional pain, illness is not accepted in the church. Many times they're enthralled with the multiple personalities. We began going to a new church and the pastor's wife started out all 'gung ho!' to want to know all about me. That felt so nice. My pastor's wife created a prayer team for me – to do warfare with some of my demonic parts and problems. We met and prayed as a team only once. She realized they didn't have enough knowledge to be doing that, so she backed way off. She had wanted me to be a quick fix. And when I wasn't all better after that prayer session she got upset – like it was all my fault and I must *want* to still be sick...I'm not safe there, not safe there at all. I was beginning to feel safe until the pastor's wife got so negative with me because I am still in process! She won't accept the fact that working through this horrendous past is going to take time.

Lack of patience. While many of the examples already given show a lack of patience and understanding on the part of someone within the church, Lacey experienced this very explicitly.

> One time I called a friend when I was having heavy spiritual warfare
> – and as she prayed for me she prayed that I would learn to stand on
> my own two feet! Well, that shows a real ignorance on her part. She
> thinks that being vulnerable and asking for help is a sin.

Move the Offender

It is no disrespect for a church to remove an offending pastor, but it doesn't seem to have happened much for our survivors. It *is* an action which protects our children, and a child's life must be given precedence. We read a lot of accusations in the press that offending pastors are merely moved on to a new location with no reprisals. This was true in Frank's case.

> The elder arranged for the preacher to simply take another call. I
> heard that the preacher went to a school somewhere and taught and
> was asked to leave from there, suddenly was whisked away. And
> then there was something about another problem at his next job.
> Apparently he's been passed on from position to position quietly.

Rightly, Martin saw the church moving the offender as denial of the offense. Even though his church sent the abusing pastor to a psychiatrist, they didn't go far enough in recognizing that pedophilia is usually not curable.

> The Church denied it. Just like they denied it to the point where
> they'd send him to a psychiatrist, but send him out in a
> reassignment. As far as abusive power, today I view the Church as
> the real criminal in this. The priest was enabled by the Church to
> abuse as many as he did.

Moving the offending pastor has been a common reaction by many churches to reports of pastoral abuse. It is a form of denial caused by ignorance of both the effects of abuse upon the victim and the pathology of the perpetrator. This ignorance must be addressed so we are treating people compassionately, as God requires of us. It is no service to either the victim or abuser to "sweep it under the rug."

This is not to say that the church never responded in a kind and comforting way. It did, sometimes. These positive responses are extremely important as they show some of the ways the church can be sensitive to and help survivors.

Positive Responses

In some cases, the responses of pastors or others in the church *were* positive, offering support and encouragement. Even when they had no experience with abuse issues, there was compassion. These responses could be interpreted as support, both verbally and physically, with words, presence and services.

Verbal Support

As survivors attempt to deal with their abuse issues, some need to relate what has happened. It is one way they can begin to let go of the feelings of shame and of guilt that the abuse had to have been their fault. Abuse victims are often told that it won't do any good for them to tell, for no one will listen and believe them anyway. So to have someone actually listen and be supportive is extremely important. Some of our interviewees stated that just being able to talk with us and having someone listen was a great step in their healing. Sometimes interviewees found immense support from pastors who probably didn't know what to do or say, but simply listened and were compassionate. Martin related an experience as he talked to a priest:

> I came out with the story about the abusive priest and the really neat thing happened then. I talked to this guy for almost an hour and a half. And he just looked at me and said, "I'm so sorry." He came out and said that, and I realized how much I like that guy. He did the right thing.

Survivors also need validation of their feelings. Monique went back to see her childhood pastor, who also listened and believed. She later saw another minister who validated her feelings of anger.

> I went back to see him, and I told him what had happened to me as a child. I didn't know how he would receive it, but he heard me, and he said he believed me. I cried a little bit, and said it was nice to see he would care. And I remember telling another minister, "I am really angry at God – if there even is a God. I am pissed." And he said that that's okay. You know, God could take the anger, and it's appropriate.

Sometimes everyday things in a church service are upsetting to survivors because of their backgrounds of abuse. Words or ideas may reinforce things said by their abusers and bring back terrifying memories. Anne found validation in a slightly different, but nevertheless very important, way from her pastor than did Martin and Monique. She talked about his support and acceptance of her.

> I found comfort in going to Reverend Scott and having him just listen to me and validate a lot of the things that were never validated. Being able to go to him and say, "I don't want to read that liturgy again out of the back of the Psalter Hymnal." And hearing him say, "I understand what that means to you, Anne. No, we won't." Having a pastor who realizes the enormous impact that this has on a person's life and being there to support them. But he's so accepting. And he doesn't preach forgiveness and he doesn't push God on you. He just lets God lead you.

Friendships are important to all of us, but especially so when you feel very little self esteem and are trying to heal from horrific experiences. Jane's minister recognized her need of acceptance and friendship. It was a sermon by him which told her it was safe to disclose.

> When I finally did tell somebody about the abuse, the first person was my minister. He was not just the minister at the small church that I've been at, he was more like a friend. I mean, he would call me and say. "Hi, this is John." He didn't call me and say, "Hi, this is Reverend so and so." I don't remember exactly what it was but I do know that one of his sermons talking about living behind this wall and pretending was one of the things that made me look at my life and say that I was living this lie – this life of pretend.

Brianna searched and searched for a denomination and church which would accept her as she was, and finally found one. She was validated by her new pastor during her confirmation.

> I have joined, was just confirmed in, a Congregational church. I find their beliefs to fit nicely with mine. There is acceptance of differences and a much more liberal attitude. I have even accepted a nomination to be on the Sunday School board. I have come a long way, baby! As a matter of fact that is exactly what the pastor said during my confirmation!

Physical Support

Monique related another instance of a pastor who dared to become involved, showing up in court to be supportive for her sister-in-law when the brother-in-law was on trial for abusing their children. He was a pastor who was willing to do whatever he could for his parishioners.

We were there the day of the trial, supporting those little boys who had to testify against their dad. But her minister came and sat behind us. And when she was on the stand being cross-examined he just got rudely upset behind us. I finally looked around and said, "Shh." And so then he sent a little note up, "Sorry, I guess my humanity showed through." And I just thought he was a neat guy when he was there. Every day he was really supportive. He told Sara that if George had been found not guilty, visitation would have been required. There was no way of them turning those two boys over again to be sexually abused. And he said to her, "We have missionaries all over the world. I'm sure we could send you somewhere." And I just thought, "Cool!" I mean, he dared to get involved. He dared to take a stand. He dared to care. And it wasn't like he was saying George was the scum of the earth, he wasn't. You know, George has his pain and his story. But still, it was just neat.

Trained Lay Persons

Some churches have trained lay persons to help in the support process for problematic areas. One example of such a program is Stephen Ministries, an international outreach program based in St. Louis, Missouri, that trains lay people to give support to those in personal crisis. Trainees get 50 hours of training, learning things like listening skills. Pastors use the volunteers to intervene when they feel unqualified or just need extra help. Heather related her church's use of Stephen Ministry volunteers.

That is where they take lay people, and they empower them to listen. So if the preacher or the pastor has a problem that he is not qualified for, he can call upon one of these lay people or a Stephen Minister who is trained to go and talk to the person. He will turn that person over to somebody who is trained in how to bring God into this. It's not a social work or a psych, you know, group therapy or anything like that, it's someone who will listen, and bring God into this.

Sometimes the support is there and we don't know it until we finally admit and accept it. Bonnie's support came from a prayer warrior in her church.

> And there's some really neat people that are prayer warriors. Okay, about three weeks ago I went, and I realized for the first time, that I was in fear of my life when I was growing up. It just really hit me. And I mentioned that to the main person there, and he prayed with me. And he prayed that all the fiery darts that were hurled at me by my parents would leave and go into the pit and to break relationships and holds that my parents had on my life. And that night it was like the Lord did spiritual surgery on me. I haven't been the same since.

Forgiveness

Many churches perpetuate the idea that, when wronged, a person should "forgive and forget." However, Fred Keene[17] researched the Bible and found it contained three criteria for forgiveness that reflect the Biblical context: 1) an admittance of the offending act by the offender; 2) repentance, that is the perpetrator must not only say he or she is sorry, but also no longer have the power to repeat the offending behavior; and 3) justice for the person harmed, which must include necessary equalization of power between the parties – either an empowerment of the wronged, or a decrease or removal of power for the person who has abused it. "There is no instance in the New Testament of a person's being 'forgiven' by someone lower in the power hierarchy...Only someone with greater power in the relationship could perform an act of forgiveness" (p. 34).

Like many survivors, Jessica had struggled with the concept of forgiveness of her abuser father. How does one forgive when the abuser won't even admit wrongdoing? Her pastor responded to her concerns with insight into her frustrations and the forgiveness issue.

> My dad was dying and I thought, all he has to do is say "forgive me" and he's forgiven and everything's fine. And that bothered me. I can say I'm glad I'm going to be forgiven for my sins, but I can't quite swallow this that he's going to get off scott free. That all he has to do is say "please forgive me" and everything's done. And I went in and talked to the pastor about that – and I said I felt really bad because I'm supposed to forgive my parents and my family for what they did but I can't do that right now, I'm not to that point yet. But when I told him that, he asked me, "Well, do you want your father to

go to hell?" And I said, "No, I really don't. But I want him somehow
to pay – not hell." And then, you know I kind of feel guilty about
that too. And I said to the pastor, "And then I feel like it makes me a
bad person." And he said, "Jessica, I don't think so. You say you
really don't want your father to go to hell. "Your feelings are
understandable." And he said, "God understands." I hope so.

Another time the forgiveness issue led to her revealing her multiplicity,
all the while fearing reprisal.

> When I had a problem with one of the sermons on forgiveness I said I
> couldn't go back to church until I get my questions answered. I
> decided to go for it; I was going to get real brave because I had a
> friend who was also multiple and the church found out and kicked
> her out, saying she had the devil inside her. I said, "You can kick me
> out now, I won't even go here anymore. I'm just going to lay it right
> on the table." And I told him and he said, "You're not the only one;
> we have another multiple in the church." And I said, "You're not
> going to make me go away?" And he said, "No, God loves you too."

For some survivors, the churches need to understand the trauma
they present when asking an abuse survivor to forgive his or her abuser.
In fact, Maggie pleaded:

> Stop saying, "Forgive." Stop saying, "Forgive." If they just did that,
> then I think maybe they could do some good work. They should
> always say, "You don't ever have to forgive. If it comes, it will come;
> you don't have to forgive." They should always say that. I mean
> forgiveness is something that happens to you. It's not something
> that you choose to do. They don't know that. Those churches don't
> know that yet. If they tell the victim, at any point in time, that they
> have to forgive, then they are abusing the person more, and churches
> are doing more damage.

Sermons

Pastors have an invaluable tool at hand to show survivors they are
accepted; they can use the pulpit to let people know how they feel
about an issue, and preach for or against it. Sarah found some church
sermons to be very supportive. Was that her priest's way of letting her
know he knew of her troubles?

> I went to church because that was really my outlet. That was the
> only place I could go. At least my husband let me go to church. But

there were several times in different sermons that something hit home and it was just like this is a Godsend. It was talking about people controlling other people, and I began to realize. I never let go of my faith, and still I thought it was like sometimes He sent messages almost.

Unanticipated Sources

Response of the church doesn't have to involve the pastor. Sometimes the most appreciated reactions come from others within the congregation – from sources completely unanticipated. Sarah found support from one such source within her church:

> By the last child one of the nuns that was interviewing for baptism, the classes and stuff, she says, "If that was my sister, I would make it out now. I know you're Catholic and you don't believe in divorce, but nobody can live in an abusive situation." She says, "That's not the way it's intended to be." She was willing to help me all the way. I'm sure I could have moved in with them if I wanted to, because she was really concerned. She said, "I can't let that go on like that." She tried contacting me in various ways that I would get out, and just was willing to help me.

Webster's New World Dictionary defines "Christian" as "a decent, respectable person...having the qualities demonstrated and taught by Jesus Christ, as love, kindness, humility, etc." Michael found solace at church as a child in an unsuspecting way from truly Christian women who were kind to him even though he was acting out and not necessarily a nice little boy at that time.

> I remember the things at church too, and if there is anything really that helped me through that time, it was that there were very nice people at church who were nobodies, who were still very nice to me. I remember quite a number, and more so not necessarily the men, but a number of the women of the church who would always take time for the kids in the church and talk to them and be nice to them. I have some very fond memories of those people at church, and as far as a good feeling about what went on, that's where it came from more than anything else.

Counseling Funds

One way that churches can help survivors is to set up a fund to help pay counseling fees for victims who can't afford it themselves. Several of our interviewees reported that church leaders arranged for or offered to help pay for counseling for either the victim or the offender. Maureen, a victim of spousal abuse, related:

> My husband went to talk to the pastor one time, and he said, "We have a program that if you need counseling and you can't afford it, we'll give you the money for it."

Frank's story is both positive and negative. First of all, the church leader believed his story, but while the church arranged for his counseling, it was just for a couple of times:

> When I went to college, a friend called a leader in the church, and he brought me back from college and talked to me about this and I told him what had happened. He at that point believed it and number one arranged for me to see a counselor. I believe I saw this guy twice; I think that the feeling was, that was sufficient, I mean on everybody's part.

It is important for pastors to recognize when they are not trained to counsel an abuse survivor. In these cases the clergy can be most helpful by referring the person to someone trained or experienced in working with abuse issues. Elizabeth's pastor recognized that he didn't have the skills to counsel her appropriately, so he arranged for her to get counseling outside the church.

> The church really didn't have anything to do with it, except for the fact that they said, "Go ahead and get counseling" and they would pay for it. He didn't know anything about how to help me. He said, "That's not my strong point at all. I don't know what to do. You can tell me what you want, but I am not going to be able to help you at all." The church didn't do it so much as they were supportive.

Removal of an Offending Pastor

In recent years there have been many accounts in the press of churches or even whole denominations where an abusing pastor was just quietly moved to another church. This was not the case for several of our interviewees. Melissa investigated allegations of other abuse by her pastor before contacting an attorney in her denomination who would eventually represent her in an eccleastical trial against her abusing pastor. The church, upon seeing her evidence, charged him with moral misconduct. The pastor was eventually deposed. She remained with that congregation, which became split between support of her and support of the offending pastor. While the response of some church members who supported the abuser was very disappointing, she felt very validated by the deposal.

> I think what my Classis did about my abuser was wonderful. It basically came down and said to him, "We don't believe you. We think you did this. And because you did it and you're so deeply in denial, we have no choice except to throw you out of office."

Erica had a similar experience and reported, "The church eventually confronted the abusing pastor and ousted him, which helped to bring healing and closure." As was seen earlier in this chapter, however, these positive responses about abusing pastors were in the minority.

In conclusion, negative responses of the church included disinterest, rejection of the victim, denial that the victim had been wronged, physical violence, lack of patience, and the act of quietly moving an offending pastor out of the victim's congregation and on to a new assignment elsewhere to abuse again. Positive responses involved supporting the victim and helping them see what had happened was not their fault; positive reactions were felt through people listening, supportive sermons, physical and monetary support, and removal of the offending pastor.

All of us, but especially the church, must accept that some people do horrific things to others. Those offenders follow no specific lines of socio-economic status and can even be people sitting next to us in the church pew. We must learn how to respond, removing the denial obstacle into which survivors so often run – responding which can be as simple as intoning that you believe and care, and you will help them find someone to talk to about it. The church enjoys and promotes a reputation of being a safe place. It must make a conscious effort to be living up to that reputation and this chapter has given some positive suggestions of how to begin.

Chapter 4

They Pay, You Pay, We All Pay: The Effects of Abuse on the Victim

And every time this pastor kept coming back to me, I'd think, "I can't do this again." And yet, I couldn't stop it either. And so then, of course, the guilt becomes worse. I had a lot of guilt. I was always the sinner. I was always the one who was doing something wrong in God's eyes; it was never him. And I had no faith in terms of changing. I gave up the whole idea of a new creation. Once a whore; always a whore. Melissa

In the previous chapters we have examined the various forms of abuse. Abuse by the hands of parents, siblings, family friends, ministers, spouses, and strangers; many times under the cloak of religion. And as tragic as these stories are, they are only about one-third of our survivors' stories. The full story involves not only disclosing of the nature of abuse and identifying the perpetrators; it includes an understanding of the effects and of recovery.

In this chapter we will look at the effects associated with abuse. These effects fall into five major categories: 1) increased fears and anxieties, 2) an altered sense of self and self-esteem, 3) church as an unsure foundation, 4) changes and constraints in behavior, and 5) strained and lost familial relationships. It is important to acknowledge these effects, for they last much longer than the bruises and the bodily aches and pains associated with victimization. We will look at each area, beginning with "increased fears and anxieties."

43

Fears and Anxieties

Fears and anxieties become a natural part of the abuse victim's life. The fears and anxieties experienced by several of our survivors were caused by the anticipation of something unpleasant, the awareness of danger, or the intense reluctance to face a person or situation associated with their abuse. The fears and anxieties fell into five general categories: nightmares, fear of not being believed, fear of discovery, fear of continuing cycle of abuse, and fear for life.

Nightmares

Supposedly, nightmares are universal experiences. In that sense, they would not be a direct effect of abuse. Yet there is a way in which abuse is nightmarish in itself and might intensify an abuse victim's nightmares. Lydia's experience with nightmares is a typical example of how some survivors first begin to remember the details of the victimization.

About three years ago I started having nightmares and they were of a sexual abuse and it was so real that I knew that it was real and that's when these different things came back to me. The physical abuse came back and the sexual abuse by my father. When the nightmares started I made an appointment to see a therapist, and through therapy more and more stared coming out and I started to have more nightmares; that's when I finally went to my brothers and they had said that they had been going to therapy for about two years, each of them, and neither of them knew that the other was going.

For some, the nightmares were short-lived; for others, once they started they became more and more troubling. When they became troubling some had to seek professional help, like Lydia; others, like Michael, sought out inner strength to deal with the recurring dreams.

Slowly, I guess, over those years, the memories came back and I can remember consciously finding the only way I could deal with the nightmares. It was getting bad, in terms of I just didn't want to go to bed at night, I was so afraid I would dream again. I finally thought, what's the worst that could happen? I'm just gonna live it. In a way I longed to relive what happened. And that's how I finally dealt with it. By the time I was fifteen, I had a memory of the abuse, but it was still a controlled memory that it had happened, but I was bound and determined not to remember any details. So when I remembered, something would trigger it; when the nightmares would come, I would sit and think and I would allow myself to think about what had happened because I had come to a conclusion: I couldn't stop the nightmare. While he was inside me, I had to let him finish. I couldn't stop the nightmare, I guess, until I had lived through it because that was the only way I could do it. Because it was over and I could at least make sure it's done. In that way I guess I learned how to deal with it.

Fear of Not Being Believed

Ryan, Beatrice and Maggie each expressed anxieties related to fears of not being believed when they were telling their stories of abuse. Maggie's experience came when she first discovered her abuse:

> When I found out about my abuse my younger sister said, "Who would you like to tell?" I said, "All those people that think that Dad is such a wonderful man, THEM."

Beatrice's fears of not being believed were planted by her abuser, a family friend who was also a minister.

> "Well, nobody's gonna believe you." You know, "I'm a minister, I don't do anything wrong. I do what is right." That kind of thing. You know, "Go ahead, say what you want, but you're gonna make a fool of yourself." That's kind of how I must have perceived it back then. It was when I was either eight or nine.

But for Ryan, his feelings of fear came during the interview process itself.

> I feel right now kind of light headed, like I'm dissociated. I'm pretty scared that you're not going to believe what I'm telling you and that this is not painful.

Jane related an anecdote that illustrates why some survivors stopped telling their stories. Rather than an unrealized concern for not being believed, Jane had learned from experience that children were not to be believed.

> The two of us were in the bathtub together and my aunt had come into the bathroom and I said something about tongues in vaginas. My aunt asked a question and I said something like, "Well, my dad

does that" or something to that effect. And it was just totally, "Oh,
no, that doesn't happen" or "No, that's not true" and that was it.
Nothing ever was said again.

Fear of Discovery

For Michael, a very real fear was that others would find out about
his abuse. Having someone find out about something so painful was,
in many ways, like having to relive the experiences all over again. "I
was afraid somebody would look at me and just know what was going
on – and somehow i knew it wasn't right."

Fear of Continuing Cycle of Abuse

A common fear of abused people is that they too will act abusively,
especially to persons dear to them. Jessica expressed this fear:

> One of my fears had been and still is that I abused our kids. They
> assured me that I haven't. And some days I believe them and other
> days I really wonder and I think...you know, you hear all the reports
> of abuse that keeps going on and on and one of my questions is,
> "What if I was so horrible to them that they did the same thing that I
> did and repressed it or they're multiple themselves?" And my doctor
> keeps saying, "You could go on and on with that and get in a whole
> lot of trouble. No," he said, "I don't think so." And he has talked
> with my kids. All in all I think we have a pretty open relationship.

Maggie's fear is not so much that she abused her own children, but
that her children may have also been abused.

> I have fears now that my children were sexually abused. I can't stand
> it. I have to do my work so that we can stop this from going from
> generation to generation to generation.

Fear for Life

Sarah, a victim of spousal abuse, feared for her and her children's
lives. In answer to the question about some of the things holding her
from leaving, she said:

> Fear. Yeah, because he threatened me. He tried to kill me. So I
> thought, gee, if I leave and he catches me, I'd be dead. There were a
> couple of times I thought that I wasn't going to live to see tomorrow.

It was like I didn't want to upset him. That was kind of foolish when I think about it, but when you're so fearful that you fear for your life and your children's lives, you begin to think, "I'd better not do anything to provoke him."

Anne's fear for her life was based on a very real impression that she was going to die young because of her not wanting to passively accept her father's abusive behavior.

The commandment was used "honor your mother and father or you'll die young." It was a threat. It was not a promise. I never thought I had a future. I always thought I was going to die. There was always a subtle threat of my death.

Self and Self-Esteem

The effects of abuse upon the "self " and the self-esteem of abuse survivors are far reaching and complex. As the "self" and self-esteem become threatened by abuse, the body either protects itself or becomes damaged. The accounts of these survivors describe repressed memories and the manifestation of Dissociative Identity Disorder (multiple personalities) as protection of "self" and negative or bad feelings as manifestations of damaged self-esteem.

Memories

One effect of abuse is the compartmentalizing of memory. Childhood memories of a person abused as a child are often mixed with pain. This mixture of painful memories and happy occasions leads to the compartmentalizing of memories – or sometimes, the absence of memories. Michael's story is an example of this effect on memory.

In a way I feel bad because I have very few memories of anything in my childhood before I was twelve or thirteen, outside of the abuse. You look back at your childhood and you should remember Christmas and birthdays and stuff like that and I have memories. I remember a vacation we took and different things like that, but my childhood was not a pleasant experience for me. By the time I was about fifteen or fourteen and had developed in puberty, that's really when I started to have a hard time. I guess that's when the memories started to flood back. I don't know if I remember the intervening years, what went on. I don't think I ever actually remembered it.

Michael's story also indicates that disjointed memories may also be an effect of abuse. For Michael, as with others, the details of the abuse and of the experiences associated with telling someone at the time of the event, are sometimes unclear and hard to sort out. He continued his story:

I remember sitting in the orchard just trying to think what I could do. And I went home, but I remember I was so sore walking home. Oh, I just hurt. And all through supper I didn't say anything, but when you have that many kids in a family everybody's busy and nobody notices anyway. Evidently my mother did, because after supper she said she wanted to talk to me. She asked what the matter was. And I said, "Oh, nothing." She kept on pushing, and I said, "The teacher was mad at me at school today." "No, that wasn't it – something else." Then I started to say, and I don't know to this day if I told her who did it. I'm sure that day I knew who did it. I don't remember. I just seem to remember saying, "He hurt me, he hurt me." And I tried to explain how. And at first she didn't seem to grasp, and then she said, "Well, come in the bedroom and show me." So I came in and I pulled down my pants, and I had all bloodstains in my pants yet, in my underpants. She looked at that and she asked me quite a few questions then. I don't remember if I had told her who did it. I remember I was not going to tell anybody, because if I had told he was going to hurt me far worse. I just wanted to forget the whole thing and I remember my mother asked me a lot of questions and I don't know what I answered. I don't know if I told her that day who did it or what happened.

Jessica and Charlene both experienced repressed memories of their abuse. When Jessica was asked if she had always remembered her abuse she simply stated, "I've had it repressed."

And as Charlene talked about the effects of abuse on her memory, she described a situation not at all uncommon for abuse survivors.

Before that I didn't remember anything, nothing at all. I thought I grew up in a wonderful perfect family. I used to say to myself, I'm never going to be able to find any boys as wonderful as my brothers to get married to. And that's the way I felt about everybody in my family. Looks like I had hidden away a whole half of my life, you know...I was so proud of myself and the wonderful life I had come from and how wonderfully I was doing life now.

Whether memories are repressed or not there comes a time in the lives of many survivors for a reprieve from the memories. Latoya expresses these feelings well.

> I guess at this point I just hope that there will come a time when I will be through remembering and trying to understand what happened and why and be able to just deal with the way it is. And then be able to help others.

Dissociative Identity Disorder

Lacey, Jessica, Maureen, Monique, and Charlene each gave an account which included experiences with Dissociative Identity Disorder (DID), formerly called Multiple Personalty Disorder (MPD). For many, the changes in behaviors and memory lapses often associated with DID are confusing to not only the survivors, but to the family members and doctors, as well. Lacey spoke of her relief when she was diagnosed as having MPD.

> I was hospitalized again and the second time that I talked with my daily therapist when I was hospitalized he told me that I was MPD and that he saw me switch six different times in the course of forty-five minutes. I was really happy to get the diagnosis because it answered so many questions, because I never had memories of my life, I didn't know things that had happened; I knew I didn't have memories and so to me it answered my questions and it was really a comfort to get that diagnosis.

Jessica described how her MPD was a form of "self" protection.

> I do have multiple personality disorder because the abuse was so severe I couldn't remember. I couldn't handle it all and so because there was no one outside of myself to help me I turned, I guess, within myself and split into a lot of different people.

Monique, also, described her experience with MPD as a form of "self" protection. "The reason I'm so okay is I've been recently diagnosed as Multiple Personality Disorder."

As Charlene described her early experiences with MPD, she recounted how she was able to separate herself from the abuse.

> I was learning to split – I would be standing across the street from this building and part of me would stay across the street, sitting on a park bench and the other part of me would go into this building.

And as Maureen described her experience with MPD, she recounts the differences within her personalities.

> Of my three personalities, my little girl is only pain. The older woman, who is very bitter, has only anger. But I, I have love.

These differences, which at times have helped to insure survival, have at other times caused confusion and strained familial relationships. She continued:

> In the nights we would fight furiously. We've been fighting all night long [to see] who's going to be in control. That journal has been very important to me, because my split writes in it, too. There's a new entry in it, and it's usually very angry, very antisocial, very anti-God. Very angry. Very angry. Angry at everyone. Angry at God. Angry at men. Angry at the church. Angry at people in general. I'm frightened of that other person that I've become. She has become threatened. Several times I have found myself at the state line, leaving my family and my husband frantic, not knowing where I am. I have hurt many friends. She has hurt many friends. I have lost a lot of friends because of her. She doesn't need them. She really tried to get rid of Richard the two years she was around.

Low Self-Esteem and Bad Feelings

There is a positive connection between being an abuse victim and low self-esteem, particularly if the abuse occurred during childhood. Often, in a family of abuse, the abuser contributes directly and consistently to the low self-esteem of his or her victim. Michael talked about how his abuser used the "put-down" very effectively.

> I remember my grandfather put me down all the time. He said so many mean things to me during that period of my life that I remember very clearly. Things about being dumb. I was small for my age at that point in time. I was a little heavy and very short. I was always the shortest one in the class – probably because I was always the youngest. But he put me down all the time and he was very good at it.

Here it is difficult to say to what extent Michael's weight and height would have made him a target for the put-down in spite of the occurrence of abuse, but the fact is that such characteristics were there for the abuser to use to diminish his victim.

Sarah was a victim of spouse abuse. Her abusing husband also used put-downs.

> It started right after I was married. At first it was verbal abuse, put-downs – "I'm no good," and "I can't do this right." At first I didn't believe it, but after awhile after you're in it for so long, you start thinking, "Well, maybe he's right. I can't be the perfect person and I'm trying to meet his expectations."

Martin and Bonnie both talked of the shame associated with victimization. For Martin, the stigmatization is felt even when talking with siblings about common experiences of abuse.

> I don't know her whole story. In fact, I don't know my brother's whole story, except to say that he was raped in Mexico [by the same man who had abused Martin and Martin's sister]. We can talk about it among ourselves, but I've never been real comfortable with saying, "Give me the details." I really don't need to know. It's a thing of shame, still. Even though we were kids and we really shouldn't view it as a thing of shame, it still is.

Bonnie described her shame as "double-shame" because she was shamed by a Christian counselor for the way she handled an abusive situation.

> That was the time when I remembered that a doctor had sexually abused me, and in front of the group she reamed me up and down for bringing it up now when I was in the group rather than when it actually happened. Why didn't I say something when it happened?

Brianna, Ryan, and Maureen each told of times when they considered themselves to be at fault for their own abuse. These feelings often attributed to feeling worthless and somehow deserving of mistreatment. Brianna spoke of her feelings in this way:

> I was surviving so much. I needed to be loved. I needed to be told I was special and I was a child of God and it didn't matter if I had dirty clothes or dirty insides, that I was loved, and it didn't happen. So I

felt that there was some pressure that way, and it just reinforced all
the bad stuff that was happening, like I deserved it.

Ryan expressed his feelings when he said, "I felt that it was my fault
that he beat me up, that he dumped his rage on me. I confronted him
on that and what I perceived as religious abuse."

Maureen described how she felt at fault and felt like a "bad" kid for
finding "pleasure" in something she knew was wrong.

I was stimulated when it was going on, so I felt like I was a bad kid.
I was repulsed at the same time, but it must be my fault because it felt
good. So it was very confusing for a little, tiny eleven year old.

And for Maureen, these confusing feelings eventually led to a loss of
feelings and ultimately a clear manifestation of low self-esteem, wanting
to be dead.

And there's so many times that I can remember describing that. They
would say, "How do you feel about that?" I don't feel anything. So
many times I would write to Jerry and say, "I feel dead. I'm dead; I'm
sure of it." So many times I have even thought, "I wish he would
have killed me. I wish he would have killed me."

Maureen, however, was not the only survivor to describe a time in
their lives where they had wished to be dead. Frank also stated that he
struggled with thoughts of suicide driven by bouts of depression. And
that these struggles are ongoing.

I found that I was still struggling with chronic depression and
didn't know what to do about it. I was on medication for a while,
for depression, and it was helpful but I don't know that I made a lot
of progress. If I didn't have the hope that God is there, that God
cares, I believe that I would probably have long ago followed in my
father's footsteps and ended it...struggling with thoughts of suicide.

Church as an Unsure Foundation

Church as an unsure foundation covers three of the possible
outcomes that abuse can have on a survivor's sense of security generated
by church or religious affiliations. The outcomes covered here are:
feelings of abandonment by God, mistrust & disinterest in the church,
and altered perceptions and interpretations of Church-related imagery.

Feeling Abandoned by God

Jessica and Frank both stated that they had felt abandoned by God at the time of their abuse. Jessica's feelings were associated with her questioning of where God was. "My faith is kind of shaky at times, and I've asked where He was. How could He have let this happen?"

Frank echoed Jessica's feelings of abandonment by God at the time of his abuse. However, he also admitted that this feeling of abandonment does not easily disappear and is something he continually struggles with.

> I struggled with "Where was God when this happened? Where was God when my father put a deer rifle in his mouth? Where was God when I was in the preacher's office?" One of the struggles I've had though, is, where is God now? On many occasions I call out to Him now and ask for release and resolution. I expect God to jump in and give me that now, immediately, and I believe that God can do that. But I struggle with it. The answer doesn't always come so easily and there are times when I scream at Him, "Won't you do something about me now?"

Nicole's feelings of abandonment were closely tied to her doubts about God's existence.

> I used to skip school and I used to skip church, too. It all felt like a joke. I used to pray, I used to believe in God. I tried to, I don't know what you call it now, accept God into your life but I felt nothing, nothing. I don't know when I started to doubt there was a God. I started blaming God because He didn't let me die.

When asked if she felt that God cared for her, Latoya had this response:

> I see how He cares for my dad and I've seen it in other people's lives. But not my own. I guess I do wish that He would care and help but I don't expect it.

Mistrust and Disinterest in Church

Jessica, Ryan, Martin, Maggie, and Monique all expressed feelings of mistrust or disinterest in church as an effect of their abuse. Jessica's mistrust of church was associated with the fact that a minister abused her.

The minister that was at our church when I was growing up also abused me. If things like that are going to happen in church, why go? We went and I think one of the hardest things that I've ever done was to walk through the front door.

Ryan's mistrust of the church was associated with the fact that his abuser was a very religious person. However, his rejection of the church is not without cost.

When I confronted my dad, I can't tell you how good it felt to say that. I said, "I don't want to hear that crap, that's your God not mine." This is where I get the unacceptable. I talked about being unacceptable, and I know this in my life now that I do things to be accepted. I feel like I am a bad person and that I'm unacceptable.

Martin's mistrust was not associated with church in general, but rather with a specific kind of church.

I'm no longer Catholic. I probably never will be again. I've lost that appendage so that has a big effect. Now I worship with the Reformed church. I think I've got a good perspective on them too because I'm sort of sitting a little bit in the middle here. I see the things they are doing and it seems that they don't have the power to be abusive, like the Catholic church does.

Maggie's disinterest in the church is related to her disbelief that Christianity is the only way to salvation, and this, in her mind, is related to her abuse.

I'm really drifting away from Christianity. When I became a Christian, that was taking Jesus as my Savior and He's the only one and He's the only way to heaven. I don't believe that anymore.

Monique's disinterest in the church was also caused by her abuse. As she explains it, how we see God is directly related to how we see our parents, and in her case "God" was abusive.

When we were little kids, our first exposure to God was our parents, and when those parents are abusive, it makes sense that relationship is destroyed.

Altered Perceptions of Church-Related Imagery

Michael's and Lacey's altered perceptions of church-related imagery are directly tied to their experiences with abuse. Because Michael's abuser was male with features like Jesus (as he was taught in Sunday School), he hated Jesus.

The teacher would stick pictures of Jesus up there and he would be holding little boys, and that was the most scary thing in the world. I remember I hated it. I thought they were terrible pictures. I did not want to be held by any dark-haired bearded guy. Now that I have more memories, I remember the man that abused me had very dark hair.

In fact, Michael directed his dislike toward all men.

The idea of Jesus was not a pleasant thought to me as a kid. There is nothing comforting about it, and then the rest, you know, your father, the whole idea of an adult male – I did not like men, I did not like men around me. I was able to deal well with women; women were not necessarily a threat, but I did not like adult men around me.

For many of the same reasons, Lacey also had problems separating the image of Jesus from the image of her abuser.

My mother told us that daddy and Jesus were the same...That's really a confusing thing that I have to work through is the real Jesus. I haven't been able to pray to Jesus for a long time. *(See p. 20 for entire quote)*

The abuse victim experiences the church through his or her abuse. A sermon preached on guilt, for example, will take on unique or intensified meaning for a victim. This is what Michael reflected about preaching:

I think preachers ought to be a little careful about what they say. They gotta think about all the ramifications when they get up on the pulpit and preach. I remember we had a pastor then, and he got up on the pulpit and preached this fire, brimstone, and hell sermon on a Sunday evening. I don't know who it was directed at in the church, but about at least the thing with adultery and sex and made you even think that you are guilty, etc. I remember being really upset by the sermon because in my mind I must have just recently gone through a bout with having to deal with it. I thought, well, I'm sitting here thinking these thoughts and so I'm guilty and everything else and I'm going to hell. That's real hard to deal with.

Changes and Constraints in Behavior

The experience of abuse often necessitates a change in behavior. For some, the change occurs as one learns "how to be abused." For others, the changes in behavior are outward signs that something is not right, and still, for others, the changes in behavior occur because the abuser has restricted the movement and social outlets of the victim. From the accounts given to us by survivors, we were able to come up with a broad range of examples of how the behaviors of abuse victims are changed or constrained during and following the abuse experience. This listing is not exhaustive, but it is revealing and an indication of how great an impact abuse has upon victims and survivors.

Learning How to be Abused

Abuse provides its own socialization. One effect of abuse is the learning by the victim of how to be abused, illustrated below by Michael.

Over the next few years I know I was abused, I know that I was abused enough that I got good at it. You learn how to be raped. I mean, you learn how to let it happen so that it doesn't hurt so much. After that I knew whenever we were on the bed, I learned it, to let my mind literally leave the room; I used to fly out to the building tops. I used to want to be a bird so badly because then I could just fly out to the building tops and I could sit there and nobody could touch me and nobody could get me in the tree tops. And if it was raining out, I would go up into the corners of the bedroom and the whole time I knew what was going on but at the same time I was never really there. I could get out that way and I could escape. I remember my mind being gone a lot of times out of my body so to speak when it was going on.

In this case, coupled with abuse socialization was the learning of dissociation, how to separate body and self, a coping mechanism that allows the person to survive the pain of abuse. Sarah's recollection of spouse abuse afforded another example of abuse socialization. Sarah admitted:

I learned as I went on. I guess my background could have been a reflection of it. I became a people-pleaser. I thought if I do exactly what he says, it's going to make him happy. I learned if you can't make yourself happy, you're not going to make anyone else happy.

Christy's recount of her victimization illustrates that abuse socialization involves not only knowing the right behaviors to exhibit to decrease the level of victimization, but also involves knowing how to choose one's words carefully to avoid further abuse.

And he would always ask me questions when he molested me. Like he asked me if I liked it, or how would I like it if he brought his friends all together so they could molest me. And I couldn't say, "No, I wouldn't like that, I'd really hate it" because if I did that I was beat. And if I said, "Well, I wouldn't mind," then he would molest me again. So I always said, "I don't know."

Acting Out, Temper, Running Away

Acting out is not uncommon among abused persons. Martin and Michael described their behaviors in different ways. Martin's acting act in the form of drug abuse was a form of escape; however, his behavior also tainted his credibility as a truthful person when he told of his victimization by a priest.

He also treated me pretty cruelly from that point on [the point of confrontation], because I had stood up to him. He also made it known that I had hurt him, and I was again – the lack of credibility on my part – I was the teenage pot-head who had hurt a fine man. He said to my family that I was a pot-head, and of course my family kinda believed it, because I *was* a teenage pot-head. But they didn't realize what else was going on at the time.

Michael's terrible temper was part of his acting-out pattern.

I also started to get real naughty, I started to act out, or whatever term you want to use. I guess I developed a terrible temper. I would go along perfectly calm and quiet and then I would blow up, and to a degree I still do that today. You know, looking back now I realize I was probably trying so hard to be good and then I just couldn't take anymore because I thought I was being too good and I would just blow up. But as far as anybody around me looked, I just had a terrible temper.

His acting out was so bad that Michael said, "I went through a couple of years when I was thirteen or fourteen where I was a first-class shit."

Running away from a home of abuse is not uncommon either. In the interview, Michael said, "Then I started to run away from home. By the time I was twelve years old, I used to run. I ran away from home lots of times, and I really started to split from my family then."

Sexual difficulties

Ryan, Maggie, Jane and Charlene each expressed having sexual difficulties as a result of their abuse. For Ryan and Maggie, the difficulties came in the form of a pre-occupation with sex. As Ryan put it, sex was an outlet, but it wasn't always a pleasant escape.

I had sexual problems. I'd used sex to run away from my feelings. I chronically masturbated, I had fantasies about other women and it really bothered me, but it was just something that I felt compelled to do.

Maggie's problem with sexual behavior caused her to feel bad about herself – an added measure of abuse.

I think they hurt me so bad, I was addicted to sex. I masturbated my entire childhood. I thought that was awful and I hated it. It was like an addiction. I couldn't control it, and that interfered in my relationships with men.

However, for Jane and Charlene, the problem with sex was not obsession but repulsion. Jane's repulsion affected her sex life with her husband. A reality that she was confronted with not only in the privacy of her bedroom, but in the course of her occupation as well. Here she provides an example of the contradictions in her life.

It was strange leading a class on sex to all these people when I wasn't honest to them about what was going on in my life. Nobody knew that I'd been abused and my actual sex life with my husband was terrible. The abuse affected me in how I view sex, I'm sure.

Charlene's repulsion was expressed more strongly in her recounting of her victimization.

And then I started because I hated sex, I just hated it. And I would psych myself up all day long and say to myself, tonight I'm going to say it's ok, you know. But I thought that there must be something physically wrong with me because it hurt a lot when we had intercourse. It felt like sandpaper, like someone was rubbing sandpaper inside of me. So finally I got the courage to go to a gynecologist and he said nothing at all was wrong. I was really disappointed because I wanted it to be physical, but there was something inside me that knew it wasn't.

Family Secrets

The world of a child is the world of his or her family. What is right and wrong or good and bad in it is standard. When a child is abused by a family member who insists that the abuse be kept secret, the child's world becomes quite self-contained. Fear keeps the victim from testing norms outside the world of the family. Michael expressed this effect:

We used to have one of the deputy sheriffs come in and talk to us about going away with strangers and all that at school. That popped into my mind that you'd never want to go anywhere with strangers, and so I was promising up and down, because I did not want to leave my world, my safe world that I could roam in, but we never went down the road to the other kids' house. Those people were strangers. They were bad. You stayed away from them. You didn't talk to anybody else. You stayed in your world. And he kept on telling me they would take me away. People were going to take you away, and I was sweating.

Some survivors kept their abuse a secret for fear of even more punishment, not so much from their primary abuser, but at the hands of other non-abusive adults. Christy's words illustrate this concern.

I was about five and a half years old when the first incident came up. I was taking a shower that night for school, and my father came into the back bedroom. At that time he would just fondle me. He told me that if my mother found out she would be mad and I would most likely be punished, so I wasn't to say anything.

Latoya maintained her secret because she was fearful of what the news would do to an already sickly non-abusive parent. This wanting to tell but feeling a great deal of pressure not to tell put an additional strain upon an already troubled relationship.

> My relationship with my mother has been quite bad because I was
> blamed for her illness and I ended up taking care of her a lot. Trying
> to keep everything straight and calm so that she would be okay. I
> guess that's the big reason I never told my parents because I was
> afraid what it'd do to my mom and I'd get blamed for it.

Anne's family secret was kept as a matter of self preservation. As a
child, she discovered that the maintenance of valued relationships was
dependent upon her keeping her mouth shut about the things happening
to her. And later as an adult, she had a very strong sense that if she
told of her abusive experiences, she would die.

> I did try to tell my grandmother. She said, "Little girls don't talk
> like that." Then I went to my mother; she said she was going to die.
> And as far as I know, I never told anyone again, anything, ever.
> When I finally started to talk today, I was convinced that I would be
> shot. When I spoke in church a year and a half ago, I spent the next
> day waiting for someone to shoot me, literally. I think I was too
> terrified, as a child, to tell anyone.

Ironically, the child abused by a family member who insists on
secrecy sees his family world as "safe" and the outside world a place of
"strangers." Like the mythical Addams family, to the abused child his
or her family and immediate world all seem "normal." The victim's
sense of right and wrong is anchored in a dysfunctional family of
socialization. According to Michael, "It took me years to realize that
the sexual abuse was not normal."

Jessica, like Michael, also expressed how secrecy was enforced
within the family so that no one outside of the family would be aware
of what was going on. Secrecy was a necessary shield, if an abusive
family was going to appear "normal."

> The problem was it was such a big secret, everything was such a big
> secret in my family. No one talked about anything. Everything
> about our lives when I was growing up, it was a secret. Those kinds
> of things have to change.

And Sarah, in her recounting of her abusive experiences, shared how
the "normal" togetherness of marriage can become obsessive.

He just wanted to get us off into our own world and I wasn't supposed to tell anything that was going on. This was a "family secret."

Not Seeking Professional Help

Maureen and Charlene both indicated that there had been times where they had refused to seek professional counseling. In Maureen's attempt to not become the person her abuser said she was, she chose not to seek professional help.

I couldn't quite bring myself to go to a professional. That would be like making me everything he said I was: weak, stupid. All of those things.

But for Charlene, the avoidance of professional help was the avoidance of confronting her abuse.

And I would spend time during the day not really crying but with my eyes leaking sort of, saying to myself, this is really awful, I don't know what to do about it, and Jerry kept encouraging me to go to counseling, but I didn't really want to. As long as I can remember I have made up stories.

Deviant Behavior

Frank and Michael both admitted involvement in deviant, and sometimes criminal, behavior as a result of their abuse experience. For Frank, his experience with deviant behavior was not only a sign of the pain he was carrying but also a signal to himself about the true sources of his troubles.

I didn't have the emotional wherewithal any more to handle the things that came to me as a teacher. And a lot of that has to do with my past. My last day in the classroom, after I decided to leave anyway, I kind of lost it. I punched out a blackboard and broke my hand. That kind of gives a picture of the state that I was in. And I find now that it wasn't the job, it was me.

But Michael showed that another effect of abuse for victims is the generation of anti-social and criminal behavior on their part. Michael had been abused as a young child. He told this story of his own abusive behavior toward a sibling, followed by anger directed at a total stranger, a hitchhiker he almost picked up with the intent to harm.

> When I was sixteen, my only brother was two years older, and he and I never really got along. We fought from the time we were about ten years old. That Sunday noon at dinner we got into a terrible fight, terrible fight. I don't even remember what it was about. He was picking on me for something, I'm sure he was guilty completely, but we got into a terrible fight and I lost it. And I grabbed a knife, a sharp knife, and I went after him. Dad took the knife away from me and Mom told me to get out of the house. I had a red Mustang convertible that I'd started work on when I was about thirteen, fourteen, and I took off and drove around. I grabbed a bunch of clothes and I was never coming back. They told me to get out and I was going. I drove around for about an hour. I saw this kid hitchhiking along the road – he was probably about ten or eleven. For the first time I had to deal with something I hadn't dealt with before in terms of my dreams. I wanted to pick him up and I wanted to take him to the woods and I wanted to rape him. I wanted to hurt him like I was hurting so bad. And almost as soon as the thoughts go, I have to say, I also realized I couldn't ever do that to somebody else. But from that day on, that afternoon, I have to say I've lost the desire. A !ot though do.

Michael also admitted to criminal behavior that seemed a way to vent his rage. He said, "I don't want to say between those years I was an angel. I got into stealing, very much so – I always did that actually. I never got caught."

Avoidance Behavior

Avoidance behavior appeared in several forms. Sarah's and Brianna's avoidance included behavior modification so as to not incur further punishment from their abusers. For Sarah this meant doing exactly what she was told; in a sense, she was trying very hard to please her abuser – which was next to impossible. "He was very domineering and controlling. I had to do what he said or it wasn't right. I hated when he came home from work."

Brianna's behavior control also revolved around pleasing her abuser, but it took on a different form. She found that she could curtail some of her abuse by appearing "unfit."

There was not acceptance or understanding. So there was a real need to be perfect. A real need to not create any waves and don't have too much energy. I can remember playing some rock and roll music and kind of dancing in the room. Well, it was, "Brianna's got so much energy, she can do the dishes." So you learned real fast to be tired, look tired, don't look like you have any energy.

Robin and Holly described the avoidance behavior which they practice today and how it is related to their experiences of abuse as children. Robin was a forced participant in oral sex as a child. She describes her current avoidance behavior as follows:

I'm real fussy about all kinds of things I put in my mouth, textures, some flavors. I'm really aware that other people don't have those kinds of problems with stuff in their mouths...and what I notice about the effects on myself is that it's not so much a sexual disruption through my being. I have a lot of trouble with food or anything in my mouth. I want my mouth to be clean all the time. I have to talk myself into eating.

Holly's avoidance behavior is also rooted in a desire to separate herself from the things that remind her of a painful time in her life. She spoke of her experience and its effects in this way.

I was four or five years old and I did not like brussel sprouts so my mom put them in the dog dish. And my dad got up and saw them in there and he took the dog food bowl and slammed it on my plate and said, "Now eat them." I don't know how much of it I had to eat, I mean, I'm sure he didn't make me sit and eat the whole thing, but I ate dog food. I'll never forget it, and I'll never eat brussel sprouts.

Nicole's avoidance behavior was the most extreme of all the survivors who spoke of changed behaviors in order to separate themselves from either abusive people or from the things that reminded them of their victimization.

I tried to hang myself once with my jump rope. I'd seen once a person overdosed on pills, somewhere I'd seen it, so I took a bottle of aspirin and thought for sure that would do it, but it didn't.

Academic Performances

Michael and Erica each related stories which spoke of a relationship between school performance and abuse. Erica spoke of how school itself was the source of her abuse and how for the sake of a good grade, she endured it.

> I had an instructor in a class called "Office Machines," and he would lean over our backs and he would have an erection and he would lean against us during class. And if we shifted away from him, and I say "we", I observed him from being with students, he would mark our grades down. And so it was a matter of passing the course so you would just sit there and, you know, fearfully allow it. Because he would mark your grade down.

Michael illustrated how his abuse as a child was associated with deteriorating school performance.

> I had done real well in Kindergarten and I started real well in first grade -- I got mostly A's without really trying. Afterwards my grades started going downhill; by the time I was in the sixth grade I got all D's. They wanted to hold me back. When I was seven, eight, nine, ten my grades slowly went down in school. Each year was a little bit harder, I really didn't care. I remember understanding what was going on. I just didn't care. I just didn't care what the answers were. I would spend a lot of time day dreaming in class. I would just drift in class and not pay any attention there either.

In Michael's case, the abuse produced disinterest in school and a pattern of daydreaming, not dissimilar to dissociation.

The Children of Victims

Beatrice, Sarah and Maggie each described situations in which the abuse that they experienced affected them as survivors, but also affected their children. For Sarah, the effect on her child was directly related to his exposure to his mother's abuse.

> The youngest child – the second child – didn't talk. He was well past two-years old, and he grunted like he was a baby. Very primitive sounds... he was in the PPI program. Within 60 days of being in the program at the new school – they had like a trial period – they had already released him, because he had changed so

dramatically. It was like a different person. He was always talking. He was now always looking. A two-year old who looks on the ground and never looks up, there's something wrong.

But for Maggie, she was the one who was influencing her child's behavior. And in order to prevent her child from being abused in the same manner as she was, she had definite opinions on where her child could or could not go. "I said I would die before I sent our kids to a parochial school. I still feel firmly, I'm opposed to parochial schools."

Beatrice also had definite ideas about where her children could and could not go. But for Beatrice, the restrictions were associated with people rather than places; and again the restrictions were directly related to her own experiences of abuse. She confronted her father:

> And I said, "Well, I was afraid to be alone with a man in a room because of the abuse that you did to me." He didn't have anything else to say after that. I said, "The abuse wrecked my whole life. Everything that ever happened to me was because of what you did to me." And then he said, "Well, how are the kids?" And I said, "Why? You're not going to ever know them because you'll never get help. The kind of person that you are my kids will never know who you are. And my kids don't even know you exist, and they never will."

It is clear that the changes which occur in the survivors' behavior are both immediate and long lasting. Behavioral changes occur in the form of avoidance or compliance, internalization or acting out, physical or emotional. The constraints or changes in behavior not only potentially affect the survivor for life, but also affect the people who are close to the survivor.

Strained and Broken Relationships

In addition to fears and anxieties, low self-esteem, altered perceptions of church related imagery, behavior and social relationships are often negatively affected by abuse.

Family secrecy, an unwillingness to accept the reality of abuse, fear of further abuse, shame, guilt, anger, and an unwillingness or inability to forgive are all factors which strain and sometimes destroy the social relationships of abuse survivors. It is no surprise that all of the survivors who told us their stories had experienced strained or broken relationships with family members and, sometimes, with friends. Most of the descriptions of these relationships fell into three types: peers and friends, abusive family members, and non-abusive family members.

Isolation from Friends and Peers

Maggie, Sarah, and Michael each told of feeling isolated from friends and peers. For Michael, whose abuse occurred within his family, withdrawing from friends and "social things" was a way to hide from the pain of abuse.

> I guess I was bright enough or good enough that I got along with my friends although that even started to suffer quite badly – not necessarily where I was an outcast but I didn't want to do the social thing at school any more. I just wanted to draw away from everybody.

Sarah, living in a situation of spouse abuse, sensed progressive isolation from others. When the interviewer asked, "How far into the marriage was this when you were becoming increasingly isolated?" she responded:

> Well, at first it was more verbal. Then it got into more emotional. Like when the oldest child got a little bit older, I couldn't go out of the house with him. I almost had to have my soon-to-be-ex-husband's permission to do any of this. It was just like he was controlling everything I did. I couldn't do anything without his permission and I didn't know anything. He kept saying I wasn't safety conscious, that I was going to let the kids do anything they want at any time they wanted. It just got to be one thing after another.

Maggie's isolation from peers is rooted in prejudice she feels towards people who resemble her abuser. Her relationships with them are strained because there is always an element of mistrust and fear.

> I don't like white men. I'm pretty prejudiced against white men. If a man is black, I instantly trust him until there is a reason not to.

Non-Abusive Family Members

Ryan, Sarah, Maggie, Lydia, Monique and Michael each described the relationship they now have with their non-abusive family members. Michael and Monique focused upon strained and broken sibling relationships. When talking about his siblings, Michael said, "I had very few attachments to my siblings. I still don't have. My family is, in my opinion, almost pathological in a way."

Monique described not only the distance she now felt from her sisters, but also the specific event which led to the end of her relationship with them.

> She went out to dinner with them, and she called me up and said, "Monique, I cannot accept your reality." She said, "Because if it's true, I can't have anything to do with them, and if I can't have anything to do with them, I can't make it." That was the end of my relationship with Betty. All of my sisters have told me it didn't happen. They've called me one by one and said it didn't happen.

While Michael and Monique described broken sibling relationships, Ryan and Sarah commented on the alienation they felt from whole families. For Ryan, the alienation was from his family of orientation.

> I'm alienated. I don't have a family anymore. I have a younger sister, but we're not real close. It is almost like there is too much pain, almost like we push each other's buttons too much. That's how my family is now, we're divided. If it ever does come together it will be, I hope, with my brothers and sisters. I don't see any hope with my parents. I do feel like I'm the bad guy..."No matter what you do I will always love you." That is not true. I can get so-called love from my dad as long as I follow his rules and as long as I do the things my dad wants me to do and act the way he wants me to act. Then I'll be accepted into my family.

But, for Sarah, the alienation was from her in-laws, the parents and siblings of her abusive husband. When talking about his family she concisely stated, "It's just his family I don't get along with."

Another example of how relationships with non-abusive family members can become strained and broken was provided by Maggie and Ryan. Both talked about their feelings concerning their non-abusive parent. However, Ryan described discovering his anger during therapy. "At one point in my therapy I was more angry at my mom than at my dad for her letting this stuff go on."

And Maggie described the strain which can occur as a result of confronting the abusive parent or revealing the "family secret."

> She now wrote me a letter and said, "I love your father. Don't do this after he's gone." So I can't talk to her about it any more. So we have a wedge. I blamed her for a little while. I've avoided her for about a

year. We're connecting again. I always thought when I was a little kid getting abused that I was being abused because my mother wasn't good in bed. And if only my mother were more sexual it wouldn't be happening. She didn't keep us safe. I would say today she couldn't, but she didn't.

Maggie's strained relationship with her mother was not her only stressful relationship with a non-abusive family member. For during the course of her interview, when she was asked about her marriage, she stated, "I just entered my third marriage; I think that is because of my abuse." Her comment about her marriages is revealing, for it shows that abuse not only affects relationships of the past, but also future social relationships. Lydia's comments about the stress placed upon her marriage as a result of past abuse are even more revealing.

> I had a lot of anger towards my husband also because he was a male and I always felt that I was an object for him and I really didn't feel loved. And so I was really testing him a lot and I didn't tell him what was going on. I filed for divorce and it was a real, real bad time. My therapist helped both of us work through that. At the time I filed for divorce, my husband fell apart and I found out that it didn't matter what I had gone through or any thing else. It was about three months we were separated and trying to work through it all.

Abusive Family Members

Jessica, Frank, Ryan, Sarah, Maggie, Monique, Latoya, and Maureen each provided illustrative examples of the obstacles which hinder "normal" social relations between the abuse survivor and abusive family members.

Jessica and Maureen described the difficulty they had in being able to forgive their abusers. When Jessica told of the interchange with her pastor about not being able to forgive her father, the interviewer interjected with "Maybe somehow to feel the pain that you felt?" In a broken voice, Jessica replied, "Yeah. And then, you know I kind of feel guilty about that too."

Maureen's sentiments were much the same. When discussing whether her abuser should be held accountable for her acts, she had this to say:

> The sins she did, she did on purpose. She definitely knew it. And it's just hard for me to forgive her.

Frank's feelings toward his abuser border on being unable to forgive. Frank has feelings of hate and anger. As he expressed himself, he talked much about the potential destructiveness of his anger.

> I found that I can't live with anger and feelings of hate because of the effect of anger on my life, on who I am. I can't hang on to feelings of anger. But then again I don't know what to do with them and I don't know how to respond to my uncle. I don't even know if I am angry with my uncle. I guess in a way one of my fears is that if I allowed myself to be angry that anger would be terribly destructive and may destroy me.

In addition to feelings of anger, hate, and an unwillingness or inability to forgive, a number of the survivors described feelings of being uncomfortable, stressed, or belittled when around family members who were also their abusers. Ryan spoke of being uncomfortable.

> Whenever I was around my parents, especially my dad, I felt very uncomfortable. I would just freeze up and I'd have a lot of problems. I'd just go away.

Sarah spoke of the stress-filled relationship she had with her abusive husband.

> About a year after that I left him. At that time I only had the oldest child. Then he conned me into coming back. And at that time I hadn't lost my self-esteem, and I guess I was still trying to fight for control.

For Jessica, Maggie, and Monique the uncomfortable and stressed feelings were associated with confrontations they had had with family members. As Jessica talked of her confrontation with her brother, she shared how her brother felt uncomfortable around her because when he was around her, he would remember that he was once his sister's abuser.

> He won't talk to me. I confronted him a couple of years ago and he admitted everything that he did. He told me he couldn't talk to me because he has spent all of his time trying to forget everything that happened to us when we were growing up, and he wasn't about to let me or anybody else make him remember.

Maggie also talked about a confrontation she had with her brothers. "I wrote to my brothers this past year about the abuse. They both wrote me back very abusive letters."

When Latoya confronted her brothers, they were clearly non-repentant. In fact, they tried to blame Latoya for her victimization and, as if that were not enough, they denied any lasting harm was associated with their actions.

> When I was hospitalized two years ago, we ended up having a family session to try to get things out in the open and when they were confronted they basically said that it wasn't that bad and that I asked for it. It happened to a lot of girls, so it's not that big of a deal. And I should just get on with my life.

Monique's confrontation was with her father and it led to a broken relationship between the two. She described her relationship with her father as less than perfect.

> I don't have one. I confronted him. He didn't deny it. I didn't want to talk to him about it. I didn't want to because too much pain. I didn't want to be discounted.

But as Monique continued to describe her relationship with her abusive father and mother, she indicated the severity of her strained relationship with her parents. "I sued my parents." However, her decision to sue her parents is more than for her own peace of mind, to see that justice is done, it is also an action by which she hopes to help others.

> And I'm suing them , because I get to say it right out loud in front of the whole world that this man, this famous man that everyone looks up to, did this. Maybe I can encourage the other people and send the message to abusers, "Hey man. We grow up. We remember, and we sue you. You will be held accountable."

Of all the strained and broken relationships with former abusers, Maureen's story is the most dramatic in terms of how she wanted to resolve her abusive relationship. Maureen was so distressed from her relationship that she thought of permanently ending her abuse. "I tried to kill him once; somehow, I just couldn't."

Within this chapter we have examined the effect of abuse on survivors. Several areas were explored: fears and anxieties, altered senses of self and low self-esteem, church as an unsure foundation, changes and constraints in behavior, and strained and loss of social relationships. Each area yielded revelations of the pain following abuse and informed us in very concrete terms of the way in which survivors pay for the abuse visited upon them.

As we examined both the long- and short-term effects, it is clear that the long-term effects are at once real and hard to grasp. For it is entirely possible for an abuse survivor to experience low self-esteem, strained family relationships, and constraints in behavior without realizing that the root of their problems lies in a forgotten experience of abuse in early childhood. And still others may have never forgotten the memory of abuse, but because the abuse is associated with the one social institution that is to provide a moral foundation, safety and meaning for life, they perceive themselves to be abandoned by God and begin to question the meaning of their own lives.

That the survivors of abuse should pay for their own abuse certainly rings of injustice and adds insult to injury. Survivors, however, are not the only ones who pay for the abuse imposed upon them as victims. We all pay. We, the family and friends of the survivors, all pay for we are on the other side of strained and broken relationships. We, the non-victimized community, all pay with bearing the cost of over-burdened social services and service providers. We, the larger community, share in the loss of gifts and of talents gone undiscovered and uncultivated in the lives of survivors. And we, of the body of Christ, all suffer because when one member of the body hurts, the whole body suffers.

Our exploration into the effects of abuse does not complete the survivor's stories. These is more to be told. For the abuse survivor's story is not just about victimization, it is also about finding a path to healing and finding a voice.

Chapter 5

Why God?

The Abused's Attitudes Toward Religion and Church

I have never felt an all-loving, all-caring God. The only God that was ever modeled to me was the way my father modeled love for me. And that was not very good love. And I do pray, I do call out to God, but it seems much of the time like He's stone dead, He doesn't hear. Emily

The scars carried by many survivors cannot be viewed by the natural eye; the scars are carried deep within the mind and heart and affect the survivors' perspectives of God and their willingness to retain church membership. As part of their healing process, many survivors have asked God – even if they were not sure that He existed – *why?* Why God? Why did God, if he is so loving and powerful, allow this to happen? Why does this happen in the church? Why should I be a part of the church now, when it was not a help to me in my time of crisis? For the healing process to become complete, these questions have to be answered. But, as shown by our survivors, how these questions are answered is not the same for every person.

The existence and character of God is something commonly questioned by survivors of abuse. This is not to say that God was never viewed as an ally. Sometimes He was; however, it is important to hear the many and varied responses in this area. For the answers to our survivors' questions about the existence and character of God reveal not only the complexities of trying to sufficiently characterize a supernatural being, but also provide insight into the struggles of trying to reconcile the traditional conception of a *good, loving Father* God with the painful realities of abuse.

The Perception of God

Traditionally, God is characterized as all-present, all-knowing, and all-powerful; a good, loving Father who desires to save us from evil, more specifically the *evil one.* Sometimes, when the pain and hurt is great, not only is this characterization of God challenged, the very existence of God is questioned.

The Existence of God

For some survivors, God's existence is unquestionable. When Maggie responded to the question of God's existence, her reply was consistent with the traditional concept of God as a *loving father.*

> I think there's a God; He's good. I'm here for a reason and that He loves me. And His love is really unconditional. It gets sticky because that means He loves my dad and uncle, too. I know that's ok, but sometimes that's hard.

Martin, who had a Roman Catholic background and was abused by a priest, saw God as Father. However, he made a clear distinction between his Father in heaven and his Father on earth when he answered the question, "Do you think of God as a father?"

> Not as priest, but as a father. God is simply a father, that's easy to understand. You don't always understand why He's doing this, but He's a father. Don't always understand why my Dad did things, sometimes years later I did. I trust Him.

Latoya did not see God as father, nor did she doubt His existence. However, she was not sure that He could be trusted.

> I did believe there was a God but it was kind of like I thought maybe if I became His child, He would take care of me then. And when He didn't, I got kind of upset and I basically decided He really didn't care about me. But I guess because I've seen His care in other peoples' lives and I can see that He cares for others and I believe that

He's there but...I can't pray for myself, I can pray for others. I guess I just see that I'm not much in His eyes either. I don't know, I often say that if this is what He lets happen to people He cares about, I'd hate to be somebody He doesn't care about.

Maureen and Lydia did not question the existence of God, yet they would not acknowledge God as a loving *father*. For both women, it was much easier to think of God as either without gender or with feminine qualities. Lydia had this to say when asked how she viewed God.

Well, I prefer to think that God does not have a gender and if there is a gender then it sways more towards a feminine gender.

Likewise, Maureen tended to endow God with feminine qualities.

I give God a lot of female qualities...I haven't changed God in any way, but it's a God who can pick me up and understand me, and cares about me. And it makes my El Shadai so much more personal to me. God is God. Period.

Maureen's alter answered the questionnaire about God, religion, church, and family. And her alter described God as:

Rejecting, damning, unforgiving, demanding, permissive, impersonal, not comforting, and not responsive.

Her alter attached a note to the questionnaire explaining:

My body has many "parts." I am not the person who came to see you...These are *my* opinions (not necessarily those of the "management").

Frank, as well, did not question God's existence, but struggled with the concept of God as a *loving father*. In response to a question about God's love for him, he had this to say:

I don't always feel it, but He loves me in a way that I never even understood. In fact I think part of my problems have been that I don't understand what love is and I guess He's teaching me. But that certainly has been an issue, what is love, and God knows and He does it in a way that's not like Lloyd might and it's certainly not like the preacher would love me. I guess I've struggled with that

too. Is God like Lloyd? Is God like the preacher? Is He somehow
that ineffective and lonely like the preacher, and does His love
accomplish a little bit of pain in my life simply because it is not
perfect, like Lloyd's love or my father's love? That's an issue that
I've struggled with and I'm beginning to learn what love really is.

While Jane acknowledged that she also has trouble with viewing
God as father because of her experience with abuse, she did offer an
alternative view that strives to imitate relationships which have worked
for her.

I do remember in first looking back at all this abuse that I never
thought of God as a father and I guess I probably never will. Father
just doesn't bring up images that I'm familiar with. And even being
married and the father of my kids doesn't bring the right images that I
think my kids should have of a father. A father is something I don't
know and so I try to look at Him as a friend. So that's how I look at
it.

Brianna's image of God also reflects what she views to be safe. Her
words do not deny the existence of God, but clearly show that she put
more trust in her own potential than in a traditional God.

I can't see God as a man. That's very scary. So I see more of this very
just soft, floating, pillow-like substance. I really don't even
visualize as a sex or any thing, just a "higher power" seems to really
fit, almost a better Brianna kind of thing.

Monique and Christy represent a different conclusion to the question
of God's existence from what we have seen so far. In fact, these two
women represent many who come through an abusive episode doubting
God's very existence. As Monique speaks about her feelings about
God, it becomes clear that God is not a person, but rather a cheap form
of therapy.

I struggle when they talk a lot about their religious feelings. That
God has really been a rock in my life, and it's like my antenna's right
out there. I'm trying to figure out if this is a fix. Is this just another
fix? Why don't you just get glue or something? Of course, God is
cheaper, but...you know, it's good for me to be exposed to it. When
they say the Lords' prayer, I won't say "our Father." I'll say the rest
of it, but I won't say that part.

And within Christy's words we see God used as a justification for selfish and abusive behavior.

> I couldn't see how God could let this happen to me, or anybody else. God was just a symbol that my family used on me as an excuse to say, "What I'm doing is okay."

The Nearness of God

Our survivors expressed opposing viewpoints when describing their feelings about the proximity of God in their daily lives. The feeling of God being near, especially in time of trouble, was for some a great comfort and a benefit in the healing process. For others, God was not near. And His lack of proximity sometimes nourished feelings of abandonment, reinforced doubts of His existence, and contributed to feelings of having to survive without the assistance of others. Ryan and Kim are representative of those who saw God as distant. For Ryan, God is real but not active in the lives of His creation.

> God is someone who is there, it's up to me to get things done. God is watching, playing out His plan. I feel alone.

Likewise, Kim saw God as real, but non-interfering in human affairs.

> As far as I know, God's there, but I don't look to Him at all for any help and support or anything. He wasn't there...I know for some people He's the only thing that can help them through days. Sometimes I think He watches over me, and sometimes I think He goes on vacation, which is bad, but I'm more into thinking it's luck that I get through some days.

But for Michael, Anne, and Beatrice, God seemed to be close at hand, even during some of the most trying times of their lives. Michael expressed his closeness to God in terms of quiet reassurance.

> God talks back to me, not in a voice necessarily. And somehow I just feel He's there in what goes on. God has never been the storm. The storms in my life have been the devil and everything, but somehow God's always just been there very quiet – the quiet voice that just keeps on calling to me, that's always patient with me.

For Anne, God's nearness during the time of her abuse was discovered later in life, during her healing process, as the memories of abuse became harder and harder to bear.

> When I had to remember one of my memories, I said to God, "I don't want to remember. It's too awful, I just don't want to remember." And He said, "You have to." And I said, "Why?" And He said, "The abuse..." I said, "I'm going to find out I was a multiple personality or I'm going to find out I'm...I just don't want to know." And He said, "No, Anne, an angel took the abuse. I was there." And I said, "Don't let the angel remember. I don't want to know. I don't want to remember. If an angel took the abuse, fine." And He said, "No, it happened to your physical body. It's inside you and you have to know. But the angel protected your soul. I was there."

Beatrice's story is important to hear because she is reminds us that our feelings about the nearness of God can change with the passage of time.

> How do I feel about God? He's very real in my life, very. You know, He wasn't before. He didn't seem like He is now. I pray in the morning, and I pray at night, and I actually feel like He's in my life. His presence is in my life because it − a lot of times nobody else is there, and He's there. I mean He's pulled me through a lot, an awful lot.

The Mercy of God

God's mercy, seen as an undeserved act of compassion, was at times welcomed by survivors and at other times unwanted. Latoya and Nicole saw God's provision of strength to endure the pain and heartache of their abuse as an unwanted gift and His unwillingness to let them die as a dark side of mercy. Latoya expressed her feelings in this way:

> I guess, it goes back to that He gives me strength. But sometimes I wish He wouldn't, I wish He'd just take me home. I don't know why He wouldn't. [He would] if He really cared.

Nicole related a similar longing for God to have allowed her to die during the time of her abuse. Her testimony reveals that this longing can occur at any age.

I used to pray that I would die, I didn't want to wake up. Even when I was very young in grade school still I tried several times to kill myself and I think that's when I started blaming God because he didn't let me die. I should have. By rights, I should have.

Where Nicole and Latoya described God's mercy as an unwanted fact of their lives, Kim expressed her strong dislike of God's mercy being extended to her abuser.

I was like, God took him to heaven? Didn't He see? And so, it's like He obviously didn't see what my father did to me all those years. And he's in heaven, so I guess my goal now in life is to die so I can kick him down to hell. Which is real strange. It's like I'm angry at God for taking him to heaven. And he should have stayed alive maybe and I could have made living hell more than what he's getting now.

Lydia's and Holly's words, on the other hand, showed an appreciation for God's compassion working in their lives. Lydia spoke of God's compassion in terms of unmerited forgiveness, not as an abuser, but as one who acted out because of the abuse.

I have many times where I do some really stupid, rotten things. I went through a time where I was very promiscuous in our marriage and I know God forgives me for that. I don't think that God feels that I need to live up to any particular person or live up to any set standards. Wherever I am at, that's what God accepts.

Holly's testimony about the mercies of God also centered on God's forgiving nature and His love for His creation.

I don't think God's sitting looking over your shoulder waiting to pounce on you for every little thing you do and I think that was one burden that was kind of lifted off. I don't feel that way. I think God keeps track and all that kind of stuff. God loves me, just me, just because I'm me and I can make a mistake and He's still going to love me and I don't have to put on sackcloth and ashes and rip my skin in order for Him to forgive me.

God as Angry and Punishing

In the name of religion, people sometimes teach children self-serving characteristics of God. For some survivors, God was a merciful

God, even if the mercy was unwelcomed; but for many more of the survivors we spoke to, God was angry, scary, and punishing. Edna's, Melissa, Anne's, and Elizabeth's accounts of abuse and survival all described a time when they viewed God as someone who was out to hurt them or as someone who wanted to make them pay for being bad. Edna's fear of God was directly related to her fear of her own abusive father.

> Where I'm at now with my abuse is that I know that we usually view God in regards to our earthly father and I can look back now when I was growing up and know that I did project my human father's image onto how my relationship with God was. I was afraid of God even before the abuse occurred...My dad was a very quiet man, but when he did speak up it was very loud. I viewed him as an angry father. And so it enforced in me the fear that our church for a long time did preach that God was a legalistic manager, if you will. And so I viewed God as like a Judge Wapner, this guy with a gavel. And after my abuse occurred, I feared men all the more, any male semblance.

Melissa also saw God as a punisher, as someone who kept watch, looking for an opportunity to punish wrong behaviors.

> And how did God look at me? I was looking very much for the punishment. And that was what I saw in the miscarriage, of course. I was directly punished by God for doing it. I saw God as a punisher, and if you did not do the right thing, that was it. You were in trouble, and it could happen to you at any point.

Anne also felt God was someone who should be feared because He had the power to send you to hell.

> Well, I was sacred to death of God all of my life. I thought He was a judge. I thought He was writing every bad thing I ever did down. And if I went to heaven, He would have a book with everyone's name in it, but He would take one that was on the floor next to Him, which was just mine, and He would laugh at me and say, "What do you think you're doing here?" And I was convinced that I was going to go to hell no matter what I did. I was afraid of God.

Keith had conflicting feelings about God, saying "I don't as much anymore, but I used to wonder where God was as we were growing up." Then he continued,

I saw God as judgmental, bad, that I could never please in any old way. As I was growing up, I don't think I pictured myself burning in hell, but I really didn't think that I would have any place in heaven.

Elizabeth felt that God was holding her responsible for her own abuse and because she was responsible, she also had fears and dreams of going to hell.

You feel like it was your fault and God holds you responsible for what happened. Basically, I would have dreams that I was friends with the devil because I knew I wasn't going to heaven anyway. Because God didn't like me and He was a scary mean God and I didn't really want to go there anyway. I guess, to realize it, I would always have dreams that I would be in hell but it was the right place because me and the devil were chums. I know my dad brought up stuff like that, too. "You're going to hell if you're bad."

The Power of God

Traditionally God is thought to be all powerful. And Frank's comments on the characterization of God clearly echo this sentiment.

Well, it's shifting. I'm just getting the sense of the long-suffering God who cares deeply about who we are and who suffers with us. It's been a long time in developing; and I would say that I see God as all-powerful, as the Lord of Lords, as able to do whatever He will in this world with this world, but with a plan to do it in His own way, in His own time. It doesn't always fit with my time schedule and doesn't always make sense to me, but God is making all things new including me, out of love for His creation.

But for Jessica and Charlene, the power of God is often exercised through people, and for this reason, the power of God is at times limited. For Jessica, this meant that God could not control an individual's behavior.

How could He have let this happen? One of the ministers at our church kind of explained it as, we're not puppets and God is not holding the strings and telling us what to do and how to do it. He gives us the freedom to choose. If He controlled the things that my parents and my family did to me, it would basically be that we are puppets in that you know God didn't choose them to be bad people. They chose that for themselves and that helped.

For Charlene, this meant that God's work is limited to the degree that people are willing to act as His agents here on earth.

> And now this is what serving God is. It's being there for other people and it makes me really angry when, it's like, you know, we want to say that God will take care of all these things...There is such a frequent question among abused people, "Where was God in all this?" "Why didn't God rescue me?" Well I'll tell you why, because God called the church to be His arms and His voice and I don't see that we as the church are so dispensable. I think that we are another part of the equation and in my faith, we grew up with the idea that God did everything and I'm nothing, and I don't believe that any more. I don't think God can do it without us. I think God is searching and searching for people who will go on a mission of healing with Him. He's not going to do it alone. For whatever reason, I don't think He can. It takes us too, we are a part of it and the angels; it's like a trio, God and the angels and the people.

For Holly, God's power is confined to that which is good; God has no control over evil.

> I grew up with a God that lets little girls die in the street being hit by a car and now I know that God doesn't allow that, he's not in control, you know, God doesn't control that. That is Satan working. Satan has allowed sin to reign free here, so that's why drunks are on the road. God doesn't let drunks drive on the road, Satan does.

Brianna's concept of a God with limited power moved her to see God as something other than a source of strength and help.

> God was part of the problem, a big part because it was difficult to think of Him as being so powerful and yet not doing anything for me.

For the majority of the individuals whose voices we have heard, it is clear that God is a supernatural being and an integral part of their lives. However, the interpretation of God is varied. God is male, God is female, God is gender neutral, God is God. God is all powerful, God is limited, God cares, God loves, God hates, God allows, God denies, God comforts, God heals, and God understands. For those who survived their abuse with an appreciation for and a dependence upon God, God, in the words of Anne, "had to be real as, or more real than the abuse."

There is no significant correlation, at this point, between type or duration of abuse, and the characterization of God. The process of characterizing God is complex and personal; and the experience of abuse does not make the process any easier. And even though there were some who came through their abuse without an appreciation for God, a few, like Robin, were still hopeful that God was real and that a relationship with Him would make a difference in their lives.

> I'm still hopeful that I can resurrect or spare my relationship with Him, whatever it is. I'm not sure. I am aware that I'm not ready to give it up. I don't want to say good-bye to that part. I'm aware that I still communicate with Him, but not on any formal basis. I just feel hopeful.

The Characterization of Church and Religion as a Help or Hindrance in the Healing Process

While searching for the answers to the questions of why abuse has occurred in a person's life or, perhaps more importantly, while trying to figure out how to press through the pain and begin to heal, many survivors have turned to the church. For some, the church was a help in the healing process. For others, the church, more specifically, organizations of Christian believers, was a hindrance in the healing process; and for still others, certain aspects of the church were more helpful than others. What becomes clear from the accounts of these survivors is that the process of healing is often long and complex and that the church is not always a welcomed part of that process.

Help

Religion and church involvement became a significant factor in Jessica's healing process when she internalized a vision of a loving God as opposed to a God who would strike her dead for her transgressions.

> I found out God loves me. Sometimes I'm still kind of afraid to say that. I could never sing "Jesus Loves Me" because I knew He didn't and now I know He does.

Along similar lines, Ryan's assistance from religion in his healing process arose from his acknowledgment of God as a forgiving God. When asked if the church had been a source of healing in any way to him, Ryan replied:

Yeah, it has. I've had very little exposure to the church in the last
ten years. I've had more in the last two years than in the eight
previous. It was because I had gone to last Easter service that I
realized that when I can forgive myself for what I do, then I know
that I am forgiven by God. That was fostered because I went to
church and I don't remember what was said but something was said
that connected with me and it came out of that. I just felt it. A lot of
power and I just knew that this was true and at that point I also
knew that my dad, I felt, was going to go to hell because he is not
able to forgive himself. He's not really connected with himself. So
yes, it has been a source of healing in a very limited way.

Maureen considered religion and the church as significant factors not
only in her healing, but in her life.

It's really exciting. To find a Christian counselor, too, was really
important to me, because I truly believe that God made us physical,
spiritual, mental, and emotional. You can't take any one of those
apart...We're all four. If our physical hurts, our spiritual, our mental,
and our emotional are going to hurt at the same time. You can't treat
one without treating the other. Because church had become a
tremendous argument for my husband and me, I could see someone
who wasn't a Christian just saying, "Well, then don't go. [That will]
take care of that fight." But that's too important to me to leave out.

Sarah, who was supported by her church when she sought a divorce,
despite the fact that she was Catholic, viewed the church as a significant
part of her faith development and healing. When asked if the church
had helped her, Sarah replied:

Yeah, I think so. I think I became stronger in my faith, because if I
wouldn't have, I probably would have been mediocre about it. But I
had a lot of changed feelings about religion. They were positive, not
negative. That's how I was helped. I feel that that's one of the things
that got me through all of this.

Christy and Martin found religion and church involvement to be an
integral part of their restoration after they switched denominations.
Martin describes his experience in this way:

It occurs to me that the Lutheran church might very well have been
real helpful in that I felt so much a part of that church.

Christy's denominational move showed her that God was ever-present, a fact that made a big difference in her healing.

> As long as I got in foster care it was a help, a big help, because I knew God was there – I finally knew God was there. And He was helping me, and I could talk to Him anytime I felt like talking to Him, and to know that He was there, listening. It was such a relief to know that. Sometimes you can't describe it.

Brianna's second husband attended a Christian Science church, and although she did not embrace the church's entire teachings, she found some things very healing.

> It really taught me that we're not little robots of God or the devil. We do have control over what we do and we come to God willingly. God does speak to us, and that's their term for angels: our thoughts from God. That was so comforting because then I could blame my dad. He chose to do what he did. It wasn't the devil and it wasn't that God wasn't powerful enough to stop him. My dad chose to do what he did. So I found a lot of comfort in that.

Hindrance

What is for some a stepping stone, is to others a stumbling block. It becomes clear from the feelings expressed by Maggie, Beatrice, and Kim that religion and the church are not always sources of healing. Maggie's opinion of religion as a hindrance in her healing process was clear and strong.

> It was a hindrance. Organized religion has always been a hindrance. Religion says, "Forgive." Stage one: forgive. Forgive should maybe be stage twenty. So religion has always gotten in the way. I had to get away from religion to get healing.

For Kim, religion was an obstacle because abuse was an ignored topic. The church's silence on abuse colored her perspective of the church community in shades of misgivings.

> It was a major hindrance because there was nobody there and there were no sermons, no instructions or anything like that, on abuse. It's like that was just a taboo subject in the church except for the people that were non-Christian people, and so it was a big hindrance because nothing was talked about and nothing was said.

We never talked about the issues. We never talked about your body
or anything, that was something you kept hidden in; it was never,
ever talked about. And in my healing, it was definitely a detriment
to me because I was committing sins by not going to church, and I
was committing sins by not believing. That's my freedom and I
believe I can't go to church because you people don't do anything.
My father was the greatest guy that ever walked the earth to some
people, and yet, they don't know what he did. And I couldn't accept
that kind of a judgment then.

For Beatrice, religion was a hindrance because her abuser was part of
the church leadership.

When I look back on it now...during the time the abuse was
happening, it didn't help because of, you know, the minister being
one. Like I said, I hated to go to church. I hated to even be in a
church. Even when I saw a priest or a rabbi I just thought, oh, you
know.

The views of Maggie, Beatrice, and Kim are representative of the
ways in which religion and its embodiment in the church can become
obstacles for those recovering from abusive episodes. When churches
demand that victims forgive their offenders before they are ready to;
when churches pretend that abuse does not occur within the body of
Christ; and when church leaders and representatives are guilty of
abusive behaviors, and especially when they go unpunished, the
message of love and fellowship the church offers falls upon deaf ears and
acts as salt in an open wound.

Both Help and Hindrance

Michael, Charlene, Melissa, and Heather viewed religion and the
church as both a help and a hindrance to their healing process. For
them a distinction was made between the church as an organized
institution and the church as personal relationships with God and other
believers. And when talking about the church as institutionalized
religion, the church and religion were viewed as a hindrance; but, when
talking about their personal relationships with God and other believers,
religion was a help. For example, Michael stated:

I also know when I am in church I feel rather refreshed, and I do feel
accepted. Not necessarily by people, but by God, and I feel very
good about the church. As for what I feel about the church as a place

of worship, I feel very good about it. As an institution, that's not gonna serve the needs of the Christian community. Institutionalized bodies are not for the masses. And as a controlling factor in our lives, I think it should do far more than it does. I think that the church ought to take a more active role in its individual members' lives. Base it on the Christian belief – the Bible.

Charlene's statements continue along the same line.

Churches need to be (they are not now) safe places for people in pain. Organized churches and religion have not helped but Christian individuals have helped. It's a "real" relationship with God that is helping that healing process. God is no longer secondhand information, God is real to me.

Melissa had this to say in response to the question of the church as a source of healing.

Not the church, per se. If you talk about the church as people, there were certain people who were. But the church, per se, it wasn't; it was individuals within the church that were sources of healing.

And Heather found the practices of the church to be its most discomforting aspect.

The church helped me in the sense that all the catechism and all the good preaching that I have heard in the Christian Reformed Church have built my faith up. So the church itself, as a church, has always been to me a healing. The practice of the church I could throw out. But the message of the church was always there.

For three of the individuals whose statements appear above, religion as embodied by the church has been a stumbling block – a stumbling block best left alone or suffer the crushing consequences. For six others, the church has been the secure foundation which supports the healing process. However, for still others, the church and religion have both hindered and helped in the healing process. What becomes clear from these collective expressions concerning the impact of church and religion upon an individual's healing process is that the road to healing is paved with stones that both help and hinder its travelers. And that the same stones that are used to smooth the path of one, may be the very stones that prohibit another from traveling any further.

The Characterization of Current Church Involvement

The investigation into the characterization of church involvement by survivors provides a great deal of insight. Insight, not only into what types of church and church involvement create an atmosphere of comfort for survivors, but also clarification of the rationale survivors use to either continue or discontinue their involvement within the denomination of their membership at the time of their abuse. This type of investigation also reminds us that some survivors have left the church behind completely.

No Current Membership

Monique, who was raised Lutheran, is currently not affiliated with any religious denomination. And when asked if her lack of involvement was related to her abuse, she replied:

> You know, the only factor I can think of would be the abuse because it's not like I'm feeling drastically opposed to it. I went through a period of time at first where, if you'd asked me what my spirituality was, I would say, "I could sum it up in two words, pissed off." And I remember telling a minister, "I am really angry at God – if there even is a God. I am pissed."

Unlike Monique, Lydia's and Holly's lack of membership is not reflective of a soured relationship with God, but rather a distaste for organized religion. Lydia described her spiritual life:

> I still have a very active spiritual life as far as a personal spiritual life is concerned; my whole life is a spiritual journey. I try to find what fits for me and it does not involve a structured church; it does involve God but not the heavenly Father. The trinity still bothers me and predestination blows me out of the water, I still have such a problem with that.

While Holly is content with her lack of church membership, she does have some concern of what that means for her children's spiritual growth.

> Religion, I stopped going to church. I was put on church discipline, taken away from the means of grace, and I said, "Well, you can take it." I am a very religious person; I do not go to church, and in fact, I am not a Sunday worshipper. We have doubts as to how to go about being, showing our faith, how to teach our children. I mean, in the

church and stuff you have a lot of people helping support you. I want my children to know those Bible stories.

Maggie, who was raised Catholic does not see a strong correlation between her abuse and her lack of church involvement, but does suspect that her abuse may be indirectly related. The interviewer asked Maggie if she left the church because of her abuse.

If I did, it was unconscious. I left the Catholic Church because when I was a senior in high school and I was starting to like boys and go out and wanting to smooch and stuff, I said to the priest in Catechism – this was a different priest, this was a younger priest that had come to our church, there were several priests then, and he was nice – and I said, "Is kissing a sin?" He said, "Well sometimes it is and sometimes it isn't." "Okay. Tell me." He said, "If you kiss for longer than three seconds, it's a sin." And for some reason, they crossed the line with that one, and I thought, "Bull, he's just making this up. It doesn't say that in the Bible and God didn't come down and say, 'three seconds' or Mary didn't speak on a mountain." So all of a sudden I threw everything they said out. I thought, "Bull, they can make up anything they want." I mean he could have said five seconds or...He would have been much better off treating me more intelligently. He should have said, "Well, kissing leads to this..." you know. He could have given me an intelligent answer. But he was speaking to a woman. He was supposed to give her a dumb answer. He lost me. That was the end. I will never be Catholic. I think probably unconsciously it all fits together.

However, when Ryan was asked why he had left the Christian Reformed Church, his reasons were decidedly not related to his abuse.

I got married, I got out. I remember a member of the consistory called me up and said, "What do you want me to do with your church papers, your baptism papers?" I said, "You can do anything you want with them, I don't want them." And they called me a couple different times, a couple different people. I was very rebellious, I had never taken profession of faith, it never felt right for me to do that. I never signed baptismal papers. My wife had gone to a Lutheran church and they asked me if I wanted them to send the papers to that church. I said, "No. I don't need any papers." I, basically, just got married and I just quit going.

Continued Church Involvement Within the Same Denomination

Maureen, Erica, Anne, Bonnie, and Edna all reported continuing their church membership with the same denomination of which they were members at the time of their abuse. Their reasons for staying, however, varied. For Maureen, the choice to stay had to do with her love for the Christian Reformed Church (CRC), in spite of the trials she had endured. In her own words:

> I've stayed [with the CRC]. Because, you know, from church to church what they believe is what I believe. But it is all these little man-made things that I wish they could flush down the toilet – that so many times I heard from the pulpit cutting down other faiths. And that is garbage. We are all Christians. Yeah, we have our own doctrines, and we have our own way of worshipping – even in denominations you have that. But all these man-made things make me sick. And I love the Christian Reformed Church. I don't know why. It has kicked me so many times. But I love the Christian Reformed Church. I don't know why. Maybe it's because, in spite of it, it's where I found the Lord.

Anne's continued membership was more like a mission to be a catalyst for change within the church than a steadfast love for the CRC. She realized that the church could have done several things to make her path to healing easier and rationalized that if she stayed, she would be a constant reminder of a need for the church to be more responsive to the needs of abuse survivors.

> My brother was encouraging me to leave the church and I said, "No, I have to stay. They'll never change if we leave. They have to know what happened to us. Before they didn't know, but now I want to see what they do when they do know." So I stayed in the church. He left the Christian Reformed Church.

Erica decision to stay was a family decision and was based upon a sacrifice of one's own desires for the sake of family unity.

> We did decide to stay [in the CRC]. It was very difficult. But again at that time, our son and daughter who still lived at home were very involved in youth activities. We felt it would be too disruptive for our family and so we felt that we were first of all parents and wanted to stay here. It was crucial to their spiritual development that we stay as a family unit.

For Bonnie and Edna, the decision focused on the "good" people that make up the church. Bonnie's attention was drawn to the people in her past:

I haven't stopped going. And the only reason why I haven't stopped going is from way back when I was growing up, there was always one or two people in my life that I could see out there that had something I wanted. And they were members of a church. Not necessarily members of my denomination, but I knew there was something out there, and I knew that the Bible had the answers, but I didn't understand.

Edna's hope is attached to the future generations of church members.

I know there's always room for growth for my church, because people make the church. And as they get better, the people work in ministry. As they get better, we get better, the generations get better. This generational recovery has an impact on the church, because it's those generations that stay in the church.

Continued Church Involvement Within Different Denomination

Heather and Michael switched from the Christian Reformed Church to the Reformed Church. For Michael, the change in church affiliation was not abuse related.

My wife was Reformed. She comes from a fine old family that's been Reformed since the church was started in this country three-hundred and some years ago. So, when we married, it was fine with me. I'm not sure the CRC could accept a husband and wife [many] years difference (in age) and my wife was divorced.

And for Heather, the move was related to the principles of headship within the Christian family – which was indirectly related to her abuse.

The reason I left the Christian Reformed Church was when they made those wonderful announcements that the men were the head of the family and that the woman's salvation depended on the male. I looked around and decided I was doomed. I better get out.

Charlene switched from a Fundamentalist Baptist church to a Methodist church. She did not indicate that her change in church affiliations was abuse related, but did describe her change as a quest for a safe place. However, she is not sure if she will remain affiliated with the Methodist Church. When asked about her church involvement, she had this to say:

> If we can keep the momentum going, then we'll find ways to make places healing and safe, so we're still looking. Right now we've tried the Methodist church and there's some nice things about that. I don't know where we'll end up.

And like Charlene, Frank switched his church affiliation in search of a safe place. When describing why he is now affiliated with the Reformed Church of America, he had this to say:

> It is a place that I can go. Some days are rather incredible experiences lately. I can go there and experience who God is and what He says about me in His word and then I fall apart and I'm free to fall apart in the knowledge of all that. At times, it's almost like the tarantula shedding his skin. I crawl out of this crusty skin that I build up throughout the week and allow myself to stand naked before God and He says to me, "I know who you are and I know all of your failings and I love you anyway." And after such an experience I spend Sundays almost like a tarantula spends his next hour and a half or two hours after he sheds his skin. I'm not good for much, but I'm sensitive to the world, (and) to what God says about it.

Lydia went from CRC to Reformed Church of America. Her denominational journey, however, had little to do with abuse, but rather with opportunities to become a pastor.

> I left the CRC about three years ago, when I switched from a CRC seminary to a Reformed Church seminary. I went to the Reformed Church for ordination purposes. It was a little bit friendlier atmosphere for women, too. I am now Reformed.

It is apparent from the survivors' reports that decisions concerning church membership and involvement are affected by numerous factors. Factors which include, but are not limited to: abuse, feelings of safety, marital relationships, feelings of loyalty, feelings of betrayal, and time. The survivor's accounts of their continued involvement, or lack of involvement, in organized religion reminds us that sometimes the smallest things, such as telling a teenager that a kiss lasting more than three seconds is a sin, can be cause for a person to leave a denomination; and that the smallest things, such as reminding a person that God loves them, can be cause for a person to maintain a religious affiliation even when abuse has been a part of the individual's religious experience.

This chapter began with the question "*Why God?*" and we have examined how many survivors of abuse answered the question for themselves. Sometimes they accepted the explanations given by others – by those in the church. At other times, they rejected everyone's opinions but their own. For some, "*Why God?*" was answered with, "*There is no God.*" For others, "*Why God?*, was answered with, "*People are not God, and people are not perfect.*"

Chapter 6

Supportive Ventures – How the Church Can Help

Pastors, Christians must learn to trust victims of abuse and their stories. If the victim is not telling the truth, that will show in other areas of their lives -- deviant behavior in other ways. But to not believe a true victim can hinder that person's relationship to not only the church but to Jesus Christ. The church needs to hear this. The church needs to model Jesus Christ -- reach out to the hurting. In the case of victims of abuse, believe them, and help them toward healing – whatever resources you can find and give. Anita

I wish that ministers could say, "This is a safe place for you to have your anger, and God will love you even though you're angry, even though you're hurt, even though you have this shame." That message needs to be there because anger is a huge part of the healing. We have to have it. That has to be safe and acceptable. Brianna

Webster's New World Dictionary defines support as "to carry or bear the weight of; keep from falling, slipping or sinking; hold up...to give courage, faith or confidence to; help or comfort." Support is what the church needs to give to the person who has been abused.

We decided our investigation should be a balanced examination of the connection between religion and abuse. And to do this, we decided to address not only how the church and religion may contribute to abuse, but also how the church could help both to alleviate some of the pain caused by abuse and to prevent abuse. This chapter looks at survivors' responses to these questions.

We asked three questions dealing with how the church could help: 1) how the church could help abuse survivors, 2) how the church could help abusers, and 3) the qualities of an ideal church.

How the Church Can Help Survivors

As the interviewees described the ways in which the church could help survivors of abuse, five themes became apparent: recognizing the reality of abuse, accepting and listening, involvement in healing, making the church a safe place, and confronting abuse.

Recognizing the Reality of Abuse

When asked how the church could help abuse survivors, several suggested the need for the church to be more open about this problem, since the church has tended to deny and cover up. Latoya simply said: "I guess I think they should open up and stop keeping the secrecy of it." Holly took a few more words to say it:

> First, be aware that it's more prevalent in the church. The church cloaks it. I mean "the people are fine, upstanding people in the church," "people don't do that kind of stuff." I think the church has to be made aware just what is going on. Just because there are fine upstanding people and that you don't delve into this, the church doesn't want to know.

Bonnie noted that the church tends to say "Oh, it's out *there*. It's not *inside* the church" and for that reason she said the church, as a first step, needs to gain an understanding of what abuse is. Christy added that this understanding must include knowing "what harm it does to people that it happens to."

In answer to the question of how the church can help survivors, Lacey put it this way: "First of all, probably by believing that it really happens. I know of people in churches that just think that Christians couldn't *possibly* abuse their kids. So first of all believe that it happens."

Abuse, especially sexual, has been a topic difficult for the church to admit and openly speak about. On this point, Melissa commented:

In terms of dealing with sexual abuse in the church, the first thing you have to do is give people permission to speak about it. I know of actually a pastor and his wife who are on the road of recovery from sexual abuse. And not a single person in the congregation knows about it, because they are afraid that, if they share that with anyone, they're going to be ousted from the church and rejected. So the church has to get to a point were it can accept dealing with sexual abuse.

Accepting and Listening

The most frequent response to the question of how the church can help the survivor was simply accept me, believe me, and listen. Emily said it succinctly, "Just accept me the way I am, broken." Elizabeth said it this way:

I didn't feel like I had to tell them everything...Just that they know that you were abused and that they say, "We love you still." It's that simple. You know, "We still love you and we're here for you." And not, "Yeewww, boy, you shouldn't bring up this stuff we don't want to hear about." That's the way I know a lot of churches react.

But Michael also talked about a more generalized need for abuse survivors to feel included.

When a person has survived abuse, the church has to somehow let sinners become a part of the congregation. Sinners not in terms of you've done anything wrong, but we aren't all pure. I'm not pure because I was abused, and truthfully I still feel somehow I should have stopped it. I should have never been abused. And that will always be there. Personally for me there's nothing the church could do because they don't know it. If the church knew I had been abused, I would like to be treated normally. You see a handicapped person come in with his wheelchair, we accommodate maybe, in terms of making it easier to enter, but we try very hard not to stare. Don't stare at the woman or the man who's been abused. We try and include them in the activities because maybe they're a little bit shy. Maybe that's what you ought to do with the abused person too – the child who's been abused – and maybe we should make a special effort to make sure they join the activities, they feel a part and accepted.

Lacey requested that the church give survivors positive attention. "Negative attention is yucky. Who wants negative attention?" Then she added:

> I just want the church to love and accept me. And it would be wonderful if they would respect me, too. We with emotional problems are not a lesser people. We have worth, too. We usually have a lot more compassion for others because of what we have been through.

When Charlene was asked what the church could have done to help her as an abuse survivor, she emphasized just being believed.

> First of all, it needed to believe me when I came to it, to know. In the one sense I can understand that it was a cultural context in which people didn't even believe in abuse, how were they going to believe in this. But I needed to be believed.

While Frank emphasized the need for the church to be willing to listen to survivors, he also thought that it ought to teach people how to listen.

> Maybe the church needs to teach people just how to listen and how to not panic when someone falls apart in their presence. I mean the real struggle is, if someone would talk to me about what I was experiencing during the church service, someone who observed that I was falling apart, their first reaction might be panic and maybe the message that the church needs to send is, teach the people not to panic. Teach the people that we all are strugglers on the way and that what's important is that you recognize that and you just be willing to listen to someone else's struggle and not try to fix it.

Lydia focused on the point of forgiveness. Consider the following exchange between her and her interviewer, whose comments are in italics:

> I think that they really have to be more accepting, they really have to feel the pain that survivors went through. I think that they try to discount all of that.
>
> *Do you think that they don't think the pain is real because it happened so long ago or do you think that it's just that they're afraid of what that pain is like?*

I think it's because it was so long ago. "Let go of it; okay, now get on with your life."

Kind of like forgive and forget.

Yeah, but you can't just forgive and forget just because the Bible says, "Let he who is without sin cast the first stone." Yeah, I've got a lot of sin and, yeah, I'm a bad person, but I still need to have your forgiveness, no, not forgiveness, your empathy. You still have to know that I went through a lot of pain.

Brianna charged that ministers need to listen, to resist pressing for forgiveness, given the anger that is a consequence of abuse.

I think ministers are very quick to jump in with the "forgiveness" and "made to forgive." Forgiveness will not come until the anger is allowed. The anger is so natural. We weren't allowed to have it as children. Unacceptable. Totally unacceptable. And scary! You could be punished if you experienced that. And to be told in a church if you're angry and not forgiving, God will be angry. That's not fair.

Martin said he needed "more than listening," although listening was the first step, because he was struggling with feelings of revenge, anger, and guilt.

They [the church] haven't been able to get me to reconcile this revenge thing, but someday I'll be able to do that, too. But I'm looking for more than listening. I need some advice. Listening is the first step, and maybe if I were ever to approach one of these ministers, I would tell them this is what I want you to do, listen. Let them listen, and then I'd ask them for the advice. I knew things were going on when I was fourteen, fifteen, sixteen. I knew my brother was being abused. I felt funny about my sisters being abused. I feel guilty, that's one of the feelings, besides the anger, I feel guilty for not convincing my Dad to do something about it.

Involvement in Healing

Some survivors suggested that the church needs to be part of their healing process, not necessarily as a professional source. We asked specifically whether the church had been a source of healing for them; many responded negatively.

Melissa answer was: "Not the church, per se. If you talk about the church as people, there were certain people who were." Not the church per se but certain *people* in the church were a source of healing. Alyssa's observation of the church was similar: "The church itself for me was not. I mean, individual members first and then the church. It wasn't first. The church was the tail end, the *very* tail end."

One reason for people not becoming involved in a survivor's healing was suggested by Latoya when she told us: "A lot of people just don't want to get involved with someone who has been abused because it's not an easy thing." Christy, on the other hand, urged church members not to give up.

> And not to give up on anyone who acts bitter because of abuse, or who is so quiet because of abuse. They're quiet because they've been scared to death. If they're bitter, they have all this hate and they don't know where to send it. It takes time and patience. Some churches give up on certain people because they don't understand.

The church can help survivors heal by not blaming them. When asked how the church could help, Jane's immediate thought was:

> I guess acknowledging that they aren't the cause of it. Not ever blaming them. Helping them to get past what has to be done. But there are people who didn't get it out and are living with a lot of pain. And we need to still help them.

A friend is helping Emily heal through a Bible study. Admitting that accepting God's love is difficult, she recognizes that professional

therapy is necessary for healing and that the process may take a long, long time.

> We're doing a Bible study together, and she's really trying to teach me God's love, something that is completely foreign to me. Some days I can almost believe it; most days it's like she's lying to me, this cannot be true. I hope someday that I will get stronger in the love side of God. I think it's going to take continued therapy. It took 35 years to get that screwed up, it might take the next 35 to straighten me out. And, you know, it's hard going, it's very hard.

Many survivors mentioned the importance of support groups for them and others who need a place to talk and be listened to. Support groups are a natural for the church to organize and maintain, thus helping survivors heal. Michael and Sarah provided perspectives on how the church could create a supportive and healing environment for abuse survivors. For Sarah, it focused upon the support offered by related services, such as divorce support groups. Michael also talked about the need for the church to provide support groups:

> The church should provide support groups for survivors. I don't think abuse survivors should be forced into dealing with them unless they want to. I think a lot of abuse survivors are able to survive quite well without support groups. I don't put total stock in group therapy of any kind anyway. I do think the church should provide it because I think it has to be provided for in the Christian viewpoint, which means nonjudgmental of them.

Church sacraments can be altered, too, to help in survivors' healing. Heather reported how her minister uses communion:

> Our minister right now does something that to me is so healing. When we have a communion service, he stands in front of the congregation and apologizes to everybody for the hurts that the church has done, and he welcomes everybody to take communion. Come to our house for dinner. Don't sit on the sidelines. This is for you. And the apology, I think, is so important because what he's doing is he's exposing himself. We don't do that.

Churches can sometimes help in a survivor's healing by doing unordinary things, such as pay for counseling for those who cannot afford it, as Jane emphasized in the following statement about how the church can help survivors.

> Our churches need to be able to have counseling for people or pay for it for people who can't. I mean my church is not a rich church. And counseling is not inexpensive. And either the church has to offer it or help the people if they need it because families are not ok if there's abuse. And it's not just the family it's in. It's the next one and the next one and the next one. My grandfather abused my dad, my dad abused me. I haven't sexually abused my kids but I have emotionally abused my kids. And we've now got three generations. How do I make it so my kids don't do it to their kids? It's got to stop and unless you deal with it, unless you know what's going on, it just keeps going. And it's not going to get better. And so church does have to play a part.

Not every church has someone capable of providing appropriate counseling to survivors of abuse. If they do, that is wonderful, but if not, churches should be prepared with a list of therapists who are trained in the field of abuse. And if needed, the congregation should be prepared to offer some financial help or know where to refer the victim to find help to pay for the much-needed counseling.

Making the Church a Safe Place

At the beginning of this chapter, Brianna said that the church should be a safe place for the anger and the shame. Ryan talked further about it when he said:

> People need a safe place to talk about it and people have some very strong emotional ties to church; if that was a place they could come and be accepted even though they were abused, I think it would be so healing for them.

But making the church a safe place requires more than accepting, believing, and listening to abuse survivors, or even making support groups available. Making the church safe for survivors requires re-making the church's total environment so that it is safe for and supportive of them.

Because many survivors are women who have been abused by men, and many of the clergy are men, one obvious suggestion is more female clergy. Beatrice, although not directly making this recommendation, clearly indicates her struggle with male clergy.

> It's very hard to trust a man except just to try to understand maybe my perspective, a woman's perspective. And the worst thing is to be defending a man in the presence of a woman. To get a minister to see it, because being involved in that – I still have a hard time with that. Except the younger ones I tend to listen to a little bit more, thinking, "He knows what this generation is like." I think if anybody in that profession could go even to seminars or retreats or anything to get in touch with some of the feelings that we're feeling, or anything...But I don't know if I'll ever really be able to trust a minister fully.

But all clergy can contribute to the remaking of the church. Elizabeth thinks that much can change in the church through the pulpit. She suggests that appropriate sermons as well as special programs will help.

Have a sermon on it. Say, "This is wrong. A lot of people have been hurt by this," and have something ready for these people to say, "Hey, if you want to talk about this, we understand that it's a very painful thing. But it's something that hinders your view of God and you're never going to see God in a warm and loving way that you really need to see Him unless you get help for this and deal with it and put it behind you and you can see a God through new eyes." Some way you are going to have to say right out to them, "This is not the way it's supposed to be. You are suffering. You ought to come and talk about it. We'd like to help you." Even have somebody who knows what they are talking about say, "This is this the kind of behavior that..." – or even a special program; it doesn't have to be a sermon. But say, "We are going to have a special program for people who are interested in knowing more about abuse and its effect on the people in the church." If it's worded like that, maybe they'll go, because maybe they're just interested in learning what kind of effect it has. So they'll go in that way. But then have somebody there saying, "Have you felt like this? Have you felt like that? How do you see God?" Tell them how it affects. I had no idea, really. I wouldn't even admit that I was scared to death of God, or I was mad at Him, or I refused to acknowledge Him, or whatever, because of the abuse. I had no idea that my life was so screwed up because of that. So, I guess, you have to bring up symptoms, or something. Say, "Do you feel like this or that?"

Lydia also urged the church to address abuse more often from the pulpit. She said:

> That was a subject that was never preached. Maybe if some people heard it that were abusing their children...My dad always used that; my uncles used that all the time whenever we would do something: "Didn't you hear the minister last week talk about that?" That was the only thing that they would listen to and so I think that if this is addressed a little bit more and maybe talk about solutions and different alternatives so that kids are more aware of it.

Kim had the same idea when she told us:

> They could start from day one of the child and let them know over the pulpit that *nobody* has the right to violate the body, *nobody* has the right to hit them, or do anything, yell and scream at them or anything like that.

Melissa called for an advocacy process within the church, something that often is lacking or, if in policy form, is inadequate for dealing with the needs of the abused.

> The book of church order, it's got a nice judicial process, but it doesn't speak very clearly to these types of things. It doesn't even speak very clearly to the whole judicial process. But, one of the requirements before charges can be brought against a pastor, or against anyone, there have to be two witnesses. And I don't think there should be a requirement of two witnesses, because this is the kind of thing that's not committed in the presence of witnesses. That has to change. And there has to be a process. The whole judicial process has been a mess for the victim. Obviously you don't want to shift it to where the victims have so [many] rights that the person who is accused doesn't have the right to be heard, especially in case of false charges. On the other hand, this ought to be dealt with in such a way that victims aren't re-victimized either. There has to be a process which takes into account that victims of this are often so destroyed. There has to be maybe an advocacy process.

In the mind of Robin, the church makes the mistake of specializing in meeting spiritual needs, when in fact survivors have a variety of needs. Her "safe church" included dealing with all needs of the hurting person.

> The church is all a spiritual operation and if your needs aren't spiritual, they're not there to help you. That's what it feels like. But we all have needs that aren't spiritual and it seems to me that kind of help ought to be there for all of us at some point. And if the church isn't willing to provide that, I'll find it some place else.

Jane also urged the church to meet other needs, as well as spiritual, of survivors in her general statement:

> But when I look at the church as a whole, I think there's a whole lot more the Christian community could be doing for people that are hurting.

This is not to say that healing the scars of abuse has no spiritual dimension. According to Edna, spiritual healing is a must. And spiritual healing can both come from and be supported by the church.

Well, the concept of the support group that I had for a year was birthed out of the fact that I felt that unless there's a spiritual healing from sexual abuse, one really won't get better.

Thus we see that a safe place means many things to many people. For some it means being able to talk freely about their hurts. Others would like more understanding from their clergy, including sermons and other programs on abuse issues. Still others look for the church to address both spiritual *and* other needs of its members. In any case, safe means all things discussed thus far, also including accepting, listening, believing, and helping in that long process called healing.

Another definition of safe place would work toward the prevention of opportunities for abuse within the church itself. These are measures that would not directly address or meet the needs of either abused or abuser, but they would work to prevent or discourage the occurrence of abuse in the church. Although not many addressed this, we present some ideas here.

The church could institute preventive measures in places like the nursery, as Anne pointed out:

We can put some precautionary measures in the nursery and in the teachers. One of the things I want them to do is, "Should it be mandatory to teach our teachers in some respects about what to recognize, what to look for in children? How can we train the consistory?"

Martin had several suggestions for the church to follow as preventive measures:

They can set up a policy for getting the child to the bathroom. They can screen their Sunday School teachers. They should be protecting themselves from the appearance. They should seek out victims of abuse to advise them on how to go about this. There should be books out there on how to do this, there probably are. They should take that counsel.

Holly's list of preventive measures was even longer than Martin's because she felt the church should do a lot more.

I am one that believes that the church should have done a whole lot more. I'm kind of down on what the church does. Churches should have volunteers in their churches, they should be supporting every one of these people in everything that they need. Our churches don't do enough for people. They should have day care; they should have committees, for people that are in trouble, for troubled teens; they should have hotlines available; they should have programs for latchkey kids so that they can be bussed from their schools to the church. They already have insurance for this stuff because of Sunday School.

Confronting Abuse

Survivors we interviewed also called for the church to confront abuse and, when possible, remove the abused person from the abusive situation. Recognizing that abusers don't just stop without intervention, Latoya said it this way:

> They have to start dealing with the abusers because they're going to keep abusing and there's not much a victim can do to stop it. And they have to realize that it's important, when they hear of it, to get the person out of that situation.

When it is not possible to remove the abused person, then, as Jane said, "definitely make sure that they are getting help someplace and not just let them go hang in it."

To confront abuse and help the abused, the church will have to learn to read the signs of abuse. Both Jane and Kayla faulted the church for not seeing the signs. Jane told us:

> It's a problem because people pretend. Pretend – they put on a front. But there are signs and you have to look for those and when the leaders in the church are aware of what those signs are, then you will be able to help that family. And until then you're gonna have ministers who say, "Oh, I don't have that in my church." And there are some who still do that and that's pretty sad. So until the leaders and the ministers can recognize it and see – hey, there's problems there – and go digging, I mean it might be dirty, ok? They might have to hear things they don't want to hear or ask questions they really don't want to but that's because they haven't believed. I mean, I know that I can pick up on people who have been abused, sexually abused.

And Kayla shared this:

> In looking back, I guess I find it difficult to believe that anybody in our church couldn't ask questions. None of us had any psychiatric problems until we were high school students. But certainly once that started happening, and it happened over and over again, I can't

understand that someone from church didn't come and say, "Something's wrong in this family. There's something really wrong here." The church *did* help us. We were poor. We went to a Christian school because the church paid for it. It brought food to us 'cause my dad would lose his jobs. They brought us clothes. I can't say anything bad about the church that way. But it was almost like the church didn't want to get involved in what might be going on behind closed doors.

Abuse is *not* just a family problem. It is *not* something that will just go away if you turn aside. It is something which devastates boys and girls, men and women. And because of how the abuser "grooms" his or her victims, they do not have the self-esteem to escape themselves, but must be rescued. And what better rescuer than the church and Jesus Christ.

How the Church Can Help Abusers

As the survivors described the ways in which the church could help or deal with abusers, two themes became apparent: (1) demanding condemnation and (2) offering healing assistance. Demanding condemnation involves finding fault with abusive actions and working to remove the abuser from positions of church leadership, when applicable; offering healing assistance includes recognizing that the abuser is a person who is hurting and is in need of healing, too.

Demanding Condemnation

It is not surprising that some of the survivors were not willing or ready to have the church offer healing assistance to abusers. Jessica and Michael both expressed varying degrees of resistance. Jessica's reluctance was not so much strong as it was reflective of the struggles experienced by abuse survivors coming to terms with the concept of forgiveness. "The abuser? (pause) My emotions are actually mixed up on that."

But, Michael's reluctance to offer healing assistance is clearly related to the anger he feels towards his abuser. And it is evident that he strongly believes that it is the place of the church to stop abuse, even to the point of direct intervention.

At that point, you have to go in there and you should have stopped the abuser. "You're a rotten son of a bitch, and you shouldn't be anywhere a part of here." "I'm sorry, I'm sorry, I didn't mean to do it." "Sorry, there are certain things the church will not accept." And he should have been put out. He should have been shunned and put out. I could say we can forgive him, but to forgive him, you bring him back where I have to sit and see him. That's not right.

Kim was just as adamant with her answer, although at the end she had second thoughts: "They should excommunicate them. Hang them up. That's not a real Christian attitude, but – I guess I really never thought about that." Anne was straightforward: "Abusers need to be confronted and made to realize the full impact of the sin they have committed, and disciplined, for their salvation is on the line."

Also convinced that abusers must be confronted, disciplined, and called to repent, Latoya thought these could best be done within the church rather than in the courts.

I think that the church should encourage confronting the abusers. They did have me do it, but he didn't listen to me. And also as far as taking the Lord's Supper I think he should be told he cannot partake until he deals with what he has done. He needs to get help. I'm sure I could go to courts and have that done but I'm not sure if that's the right thing in a Christian society. I think the church should first do what it can. I'm not saying it's wrong to go to court, but instead of trying to hide it and make it look like the victim is the one with the problem, they have to deal with the abusers. The abusers should repent. And as long as they keep pretending and keeping the silence, it's hard for the victim to believe that they're not the ones at fault when the abusers can go on. I mean my dad has changed churches and is an elder still. My brother is very respected. You know they don't suffer anything.

Brianna urged the church to tell it like it is, to make very clear to abusers that their behavior is totally unacceptable; however, she felt they could be helped.

By helping them separate the abuse from themselves. They too need to feel some form of acceptance, and they need to be told under no uncertain terms that it is the behavior that is unacceptable. The behavior though is not part of them. They can release that. It has to be like that. It has to be. That's something that we try to teach the children, "I do not like that behavior. You may not hit." It's not, "You're bad, you're a bad boy because you hit"; it's, "The behavior is unacceptable. I will not tolerate that." And ministers need to be there to explain that, that the behavior is unacceptable.

Lacey's suggestion was clear – preach to them. There are abusers in the pew, often unknown by others. But the message should be made clear to them.

Everyone should know that this is not right to do, but it seems like people don't know that it's not right to do. Preach to them and tell them that what they are doing is wrong. I mean, just put the fear of the Lord in them. I have feelings about certain men in our church and vibes or just whatever. I just think "Oooh, I wonder what you are doing to your kids" because they get these feelings around them. We pussyfoot around these people and don't even say anything to them. Yeah, just preach to them, too.

If abusers are an official part of the church, survivors called for their removal. Martin's viewpoint follows:

If the guy's a pedophile or a sexual abuser, he should no longer be in a position to be abusive. Minister, priest, anybody, pedophile. My viewpoint is very prejudiced because of my experience, but I do not believe that is a curable disease, a curable way of thinking. I think it's a *controllable* way of thinking and I think you control it by not allowing people to do it; I think you control it by punishing people severely for doing it. I think you control it by letting them admit that they are that way and helping them learn a lifestyle that will prevent, that will just not enable them, that will keep themselves out of situations where they're abusive. So if a priest does it, he's no longer a priest. He no longer wears the collar, he doesn't have that access anymore. If a minister does it, same thing goes, no ifs, ands or buts.

But when the church itself is the abuser, that is, condones or justifies the behavior by inaction, confronting an individual member who is an abuser is unlikely. As Emily said:

I don't know how the church could help the abuser, when the church *is* the abuser. I have a good friend that's a member of the small group that I go to. Her husband is a Christian Reformed pastor, abused her and they're getting a divorce, and he's still in his church teaching and preaching to people.

Melissa too thinks the abuser should be dealt with by the church, in a "caring, compassionate community," to be held accountable in a loving way. She talked about the pastor who abused her:

A lot of people think he should be excommunicated, and he should not be allowed to worship with the church. I don't think that's right. I think what he needs is to be included in the caring, compassionate community. But, because of church policy, of course, people should say, "You've been convicted. And we accept that judgment that you are guilty. And we are going to hold you accountable to that, and even though we care about you as a Christian, we think you have to be examining your life and looking at making a confession." But that's not going to happen outside of a caring and compassionate atmosphere. And he's so angry, he won't hear that at this point. But without that atmosphere at some point, he never will hear that either. I think the abuser has to be held accountable. Someone like this should not be in a position of leadership until after a confession. I don't know if he should ever be in leadership. But the abuser has to be held accountable by the church, in a loving way.

Offering Healing Assistance

Ryan, Charlene, Maggie and Frank each described ways the church could begin to offer healing assistance to the abuser. Ryan suggested offering abusers a safe place to come forward. "Listen to them, believe them, give them comfort, tell them that they care and that they understand, just a place for these people to talk about it." Maggie, however, wanted the church to first acknowledge that abuse exists, then offer a safe place to abusers.

They could acknowledge that the problem exists. They could teach the abusers. They could teach them that it's not ok; they could teach them that the child isn't making it happen. I mean abusers think they are being seduced. They could welcome the abusers. They could protect the child from the abuser without putting either one of them out of the church. They can look at it.

Charlene thought that the starting point for a church to assist abusers is first to acknowledge that abusers may have been prior victims.

First of all, I think we have to come to terms with the fact that abusers are prior victims. If we don't want to look at that, I don't think we're going to get anywhere. And that changes our whole perspective on it because right now what I hear people saying about abusers is almost that it is fine to hate them, it's fine to lock them away; they're sleazy, they're nasty, they're mean, and we don't have to care about them...And I think the other thing we need to do before we're going to get very far into this is recognize that abuse happens along a large continuum and that all of us are on it, both as abused and abusers and if you can't look at that we're going to keep on making the poles too far apart and if I can't touch my pain, I'm sure as hell not going to be able to touch yours, you know. The reality is they don't know what it feels like to be abused. And we all know what it's like to hurt somebody else. And most of the reason we hurt is because of our own pain. It's trying to protect our own pain, I think, and if we can get that then maybe we can begin to find ways, and I don't know what the ways are, but find ways to bring abusive people into healing.

Frank echoed Charlene's concern that the church, if it is going to be effective, must realize that abusers may have been victims.

Indications are that most abusers have been abused, that most abusers attempt to work very hard at maintaining an outward indication that they are fine upstanding people in the community. If you started to deal with people who have been abused, there's an opportunity for them. All the church continues to grow toward that sense that we're all fallen people and it's ok to be fallen as long as you're working at progress. That takes away a lot of the defense mechanism that a person has to have in order to maintain an outward picture of normalcy.

For Jane, putting an abuser in jail is not what needs to be done. She said:

I don't see that putting an abuser in jail is really gonna help. He's gonna come out and do it again. He needs help in his brain. The abusers that are in the church need help from the church, too, that their actions are criminal and that things will happen if it continues, but that they need help. They need to work on this and just can't say, "Oh, I can do it." No, you can't. And I don't think that even all the praying in the world can just put it away. You have got to go back and say, "Why am I doing this, what am I doing?" I mean there has to be some real counseling to get past it so you don't do it again.

Elizabeth felt abusers need support groups just as much as abuse survivors do, although she expressed doubt about the willingness of abusers to seek help.

If they really want help, I think you could. But I don't think that
very many of them really want to be helped. That's a really hard
thing for somebody to say. I think it's easier to say you were abused
than, "I abuse people." You know, "I did this to my own daughter." I
mean, the pain that they'll have to go through is just unreal. And I
don't know very many men who would be that strong. But I don't
know. I have never met anybody that's been willing to get help.

Elizabeth also felt that support groups could have a special purpose for
abusers: understanding what they did to their victims. To the
interviewer's question "Should the church provide support groups for
the abused as well as abusers?," she responded:

Oh, yeah. And I think somewhere along the line the two should
come together. And even could help each other in groups together
so they can understand each other. I don't think the abuser is going
to ever feel really or see what a horrible thing he's doing until he
sees what it does to people.

Lydia proposed recovery or self-help groups for abusers offered by
the church because of the unlikeliness that they would on their own
seek a therapist.

There has to be something set up for abusers; there has to be some
type of recovery program, some type of a self-help group. It's not
something that you ever really outgrow or give up, it's repatterning
your life so that you no longer take out your frustration, your anger,
or whatever it is on your spouse, your child, some innocent victim.
You need to be able to recognize what it is that makes this happen
and ways to deal with it; and I think that has to come from the
church. Most of these people who are abusers feel they are justified
in doing this, so they're definitely not going to reach a point where
they're going to go to a therapist.

Bonnie, though wanting to endorse the idea of support groups for
abusers, pointed out the difficulty for abuse survivors to worship in the
same church as their unrepentant abusers. When asked about abuser
support groups, she said:

That I'm not sure is very clear. I know they need a place to heal and
to gain acceptance and all of that, and I feel sorry for the abusers
because they are living with a guilt that I don't know if I could
handle. A support group could be really good. There are support
groups for everything else – or at least there seems to be. So that

they could be built up and encouraged and supported. I don't know if the sexual abuser and the victim that has had sexual abuse done to her can develop and grow in the same church if the abuser still denies it. That's a struggle for me. If someone has sexually abused someone and then admits it and is willing to follow through and get help and really work on it...But the abuser that denies it all – I have trouble with them being in the same church that I'm worshipping in. I don't know how to deal with that at this point in time.

It is clear from the comments of these abuse survivors that the church has some responsibility to address the needs of abusers. And to do so, the church must recognize that abusers may be members of the congregation, that abusers may have been abuse victims, that abusers – when they are ready – are in need of healing, and that the church must be a safe place for abusers to come forward. However, it is also clear that as a church attempts to minister to the needs of the abuser, care must be taken to be sensitive to the feelings and needs of abuse survivors who may also be present in the congregation. We can't re-victimize the victim by ignoring or being insensitive.

The Qualities of an Ideal Church

The qualities of an ideal church are directly related to the question of how the church can help. For it is the qualities of an ideal church, as described by abuse survivors, that provide us with a guide as to how the church could present itself as a safe place and supportive place for abuse survivors. Although the responses elicited by the question were several, we were able to classify them under two themes: 1) accepting and open, and 2) supporting, sharing, and caring.

Accepting and Open

For Melissa, the ideal church is an intimate one, in the good sense.

> I think the Christian community has to get back to a point where we are intimately involved – intimately in the good sense – with one another to the point where we feel free enough to discuss what we really feel and what we really think and believe.

Doubtful of an "ideal" church, Lacey wants a church accepting of everyone and not judgmental:

I wish that everyone could be loving and accepting of everyone and not be judgmental. So I feel frustrated because I want the perfect church, but that's not going to happen yet...The ideal church. My ideal church would have a pastor who has a lot of compassion and maybe who has gone through some really difficult times to give him heart. He would be a personable person, not just a good preacher. He would be a good preacher, too, but personable, you've got to be personable; and he would teach the church not only compassion but acceptance of people. It is so okay to have physical things be wrong with you, and that's good, but it is just **not** okay to have mental things wrong. We don't even tell hardly anyone. We've gotten a little bit better; when I go in the hospital there is such a stigma with being hospitalized, with going to the nut house, and I would love to undo that stigma and I would love to just be accepted for who I am and not feel like all these expectations are on me, except I put a lot of expectations on myself, too. I don't know, it would just be a people's church filled with people that are not perfect but they don't think they are and they don't try to lord it over everyone else. Yeah, it would just be a real commoners' church.

Agreeing with Lacey, Lydia also said the ideal church would be accepting of everyone, especially of those who had gone through "terrible times."

Well, you would be accepting of everyone, accepting of people who have gone through some very terrible times. I think that it would have to be something with a real positive outlook, a very positive direction, positive reinforcement versus damnation. I would hope that a perfect church would do that to everyone, not just to me, but to every member.

Maureen spoke of the importance of acceptance, letting you be you, which she found in her own church.

Yeah, having a place. "You come here and you can be you, and we accept you. We don't care that you're you. We encourage you to be you." And that's what's so special about going in there. And you see the whole gamut. If you want to talk about dress, you see the whole gamut of dress at [my church]. From the kid who sat in front of me with a two-day-old beard, an ear-cuff, and cut-off jeans, to the gentleman in front of him who had a suit and tie. And they both during the greeting period could hug each other. That's church.

For Brianna, acceptance and openness are linked to healing and would be essential qualities of her ideal church.

I think it would be one of complete acceptance. I think that real healing comes when a person knows that they can come in with all their baggage and all of their scars and all their humiliation and all their scare and put it out there and instead of being retorted with a Biblical "Thou shalt not," that there would first be acceptance and warmth and that it's okay. "I hear what you've done. I hear your pain, and God loves you." And then you can dump the Biblical stuff on them or whatever. Walls tumble when I really feel like I can say whatever it is, some horrible, terrible thing that I've done, and I get accepted. But you have to feel accepted in the place that you're in, and that's what I need from the church: to feel accepted just the way I am, and not to be fixed. I think with acceptance, you are allowed to just move on to the next step. There's something so affirming about that, instead of, "This isn't right. You have to change that. This does not go with our code here." That's what I would like. My ideal church would be just so accepting, and then it would be just such praise for when you did change. I would like lots of hallelujahs and lots of "Praise God!" for that change, not a change of oppression, and "Thou shalt not," but just because of true acceptance.

The ideal church for Kim would be open to addressing survivorship. She said her ideal church would be:

A church for all survivors. That would probably do it. Or at least enough where they were open about it, you know about the issues and there was a group where you could openly talk about it. That would probably be it. It would have to be some addressing of survivorship.

Finally, together with acceptance, Beatrice tied in feeling safe, which her ideal church should be. She said it this way:

It would be a church where they accepted you for you, and almost as if God was the minister at the front of the church. That He would help people. He would give them hard lessons to learn, but they would learn by it. That He wasn't constantly preaching at you like a lot of the ministers are, "Don't do this, this, and this." It would be a place where you would feel safe. The church would be very safe. And that people didn't deny things. They would overlook things, and where they could really come together, and if they did something wrong, I think that they should confess and tell that they did it. The group would be forgiving.

Supporting, Sharing, and Caring

These qualities of the ideal church relate because they involve people doing for one another, bearing another's burdens. Being there for people is the way Elizabeth put it.

> I just think that the most important thing is to be open and I guess arms open to everybody in the church and to be there if you see somebody who is suffering from anything – alcoholism or lousy marriage – that you don't shy away from those people. Those are the people that need you the most. I think it's our duty, or whatever, to be there for those people. That's what the church is for, I think.

Jessica addressed the need for the membership within the church to be compassionate and able to bear one another's burdens.

> I'd have to say like my congregation. Part of it is there are a lot of people there that are hurting – and very understanding and they care. They're there to support you, to cry on your shoulder or to let you cry on theirs, whatever. A lot of the people there have gone through difficult times and I guess that's got to be ideal because that is where a lot of understanding comes from. For the love of God to show through. And I'd have a pastor that can talk to people and comfort people.

In Latoya's view, bearing one another's burdens does not remove responsibility. As she put it:

> A church where we can bear each others' burdens. People say that they shouldn't have to deal with it, but I'm not sure *I* should have to deal with it either. And I think that the Bible says we should bear each other's burdens. It's not easy but if God gives us the strength, He'll give them the strength, too. They can't go through the healing process for us, but they can support – just be willing to be there, and to listen, and not to be afraid of it to the extent that they seem to be. People often want to take responsibility for a person who has become suicidal, and it doesn't work because really the only person who can be responsible is the person themselves. And I think that's a big problem with a lot of people who try to help. They can be there for them, but they can't take responsibility.

Emily is in a group that deeply cares for each other, so her ideal church is partly realized. She told the interviewer:

> I have a small group that I get together with. We're confidential, independent, but we're all Christian Reformed Church members. And we all care very deeply about each other. I think it's important to be able to have a church that is open and understands, not be so afraid of abuse.

Supporting, sharing, and caring are important qualities for the church because it may have to serve as surrogate family. This was Bonnie's experience:

> The ideal church would be where people don't come with so many masks. Where people can share what they're going through and not get shot down for it, but be supported. And a church where there's fellowship going on. Like with myself and my sister, when we split from the family, we lost all contact of doing things with family. We just don't have it. It's like the church could pick up some of that. Like having dinners together at church, or something to be a part of a unit. I think there's a strong need for that.

For Melissa, the ideal church is a support in the time of crisis, something the church has not always done well. She told us:

> I think the church should be a place where if there's a crisis someone is there to support you. And certainly don't make the crisis worse like my church did. That's the thing we do, and I think we ignore the crises in people's lives. We had house visitation from my husband's church – we get it twice a year; we're lucky. His church came a couple of weeks ago, and we more or less said, "Your church could have been supportive to us. But instead your church turned on us also." And we'd said it nicely, and it's not so much because they did it to us, but we pointed out this is what happens in the church, and it's done to other people going through other things. And sometimes we as the church think that what we're being is Christian, but it's not.

The ideal church? Erica picked up on it being servant. She said about her ideal church:

> It would certainly get away from the hierarchical stuff of the church today. Be getting back toward recognizing the gifts that God's given to the people who have been working in areas, the giftedness,

rather than because they shimmied the hierarchical ladder. That's a big thing I think, the servant – a servant attitude of ministry rather than a power trip.

Maureen told of the spirit of love, the caring needed among the members of the church. For it is with love that the church will be able to stop hurting people. As she talked about the kind of love that's needed in the church, she retold a portion of a sermon on geese and sea gulls she had recently heard.

Just lately I heard a sermon about – the passage came from Romans – about being different parts of the body. And about the weak ones are there for the strong ones to help them. About how we need to not be sea gulls, we need to be geese. If you want to kill a sea gull, tie a red ribbon on their leg, because they'll peck it to death because it has something different. They will just absolutely kill it. Feed a sea gull; you've never seen a scrappier bird in your life. And it's true. You think about that; go out and feed a sea gull bread. They'll fight tooth and nail over one little piece of bread. And the same bird will get it every time. And if another one gets it, they'll peck at it. Geese aren't that way. Sometimes they feed it to each other. And when they're flying, the honking sends on the leader goose. If the leader goose gets tired, they go all the way to the back end, and the next strongest goose comes up. If one of them in that "V" gets tired and has to go down to the ground, at least two others go with, that are stronger than it. And how as a church we need to learn how to be geese and not sea gulls. How the weak ones are there for the strong ones to help them. Otherwise the strong ones wouldn't have a job to do.

Anne's answer to the question was succinct but powerful: "Ideal church, they're Jesus with skin on. That's what they are, they're Jesus with skin on. They just love. They don't judge you, they don't condemn you. They lead you, guide you, nurture you." In an addendum to her interview, Anne had reflected more on the question and then wrote this statement of ideal church qualities, which perhaps sums up rather well what the others have said:

I would like to see a church be honest enough to admit that sexual abuse has and is taking place in their congregation. Brave enough to address it openly, making it difficult and uncomfortable for abusers to feel safe. Caring enough to commit themselves to walking with victims of sexual abuse. Wise enough to set guidelines in place for the protection of God's precious little children that He entrusted to their care. Discerning enough to know how to handle accusations and diligent enough to hold abusers accountable.

In summary, how can the church help survivors of abuse? It can recognize the reality and existence of abuse, be accepting and listen, involve themselves in the long healing process, make the church an emotionally safe place, and confront abuse.

The church can help abusers by condemning their abusive actions and offering healing assistance. This includes preaching against abuse from the pulpit, expecting repentance, teaching abusers that their actions are not appropriate in God's kingdom, and removing the offender from church office; help can be given by recognizing that they were probably abused themselves at some time, offering counseling and support groups.

And finally, what are the qualities of an ideal church? It is different things for different people. For some, it may be the compassion of church members; for others, it may be the feeling of openness and acceptance of all types of people. But if the church is to be a place of safety and healing for all, it will have to adopt the qualities which make it an ideal place for survivors and abusers alike. And those qualities, as expressed by the abuse survivors participating in this project, are acceptance, openness, supporting, sharing, and caring. The ideal should become real.

Chapter 7

In Other Words . . .

Pay attention, and listen to the words of the wise; apply your heart to what I teach. Proverbs 22: 17 (NIV)

For several chapters now, we have been listening to the words of the many abuse survivors who interviewed with us. Each was more than willing to tell her or his story of abuse, religion, and the church. Each story was unique in its description of the relationship between abuse, religion, and the church and the impact of each upon their lives. They told their stories as part of their healing and to create awareness, for those willing to listen, about what they have learned from their experiences. Previous chapters have identified the common threads of their stories: how religion was used to justify abuse; how the church can be a blessing or a hindrance in the healing process; how God and his power are sometimes questioned; and that surviving abuse is a process which involves more than just "forgiving and forgetting."

In this chapter, we reflect upon what they have told us, and provide recommendations for action as well as a list of resources. In other words, these are the important messages we think abuse survivors want churches and synagogues to hear and put into practice.

Stop the Justification of Abuse

Survivors have told us how specific Bible verses, religious practices, and theological beliefs were used, not only by the abusers but also by others and in particular church members, to justify their abuse. Bible verses included "Wives, submit yourselves unto your own husbands," "Children, obey your parents" and that often-misquoted "Spare the rod and spoil the child." Theological beliefs which strongly emphasize people being sinners help to convince victims that they deserve the abuse and their victimizer is correct when she or he says it must be done. We talked about rules of men and women as taught by the church, rules which place men as the powerful head of all women and children; punishment from God, where abusers told their victims that God told them to inflict punishment for wrongdoing, but these statements gave the impression of a vengeful God; references to the devil, where children were demeaned, such as called the devil's daughter, thus deserving of abuse. Abuse doesn't happen in "good Christian families," is a phrase we often hear, but we found that abusing families put on a front so they only appeared to be "good Christians." The church must realize that just because a person attends church or even is active therein doesn't mean she or he is a good Christian. Be open to listening and observing. It is important for churches to realize that some teachings are very appropriate for the "normal" member, but that those same teachings can lead to more victimization of abuse survivors. Finally, the pastor who uses his or her position of authority and as a "man of God" or "woman of God" to justify abusive actions is perhaps the most awful example of abuse by the church and results in the breaking down of trust in religion and the church. The church must carefully examine the credentials of a new pastor, including past church history and why she or he is leaving a present call.

The church needs to examine its teachings to determine how concepts important to its theology can still be taught but in ways that show sensitivity to victims of abuse, known or unknown, and to others who may react differently to terminology or concepts. In addition, the church should preach about and teach self esteem to members of all ages and genders. This is not to say that the church has to stop preaching about the "sin-nature-of-man." But, it does suggest that church should insure that all of its members realize that they are image-bearers of God and, as such, are not deserving of mistreatment and abuse. Most certainly, the church and its members need to stop justifying abuse and make it clear that abuse is a sin and is always unjustified (and never the fault of the victim).

Substitute Denial with Positive Responses

Survivors told us that people in the church often do not know how to respond to abuse. From personal experience, they identified a host of negative responses: disinterest, rejection, physical violence, denial, unrealistic expectations, lack of patience, and merely moving the offender. Denial was the most common response, it seems; many of the other negative responses are simply offshoots of it. Many times we heard survivors say, "You don't know how important to my healing it is that you would both listen and believe me." So the church needs, first, to examine how denial as a first response is so damaging to an abuse victim and escalates the victimization. Denial intensifies the victimization of survivors because of the feelings of hopelessness, isolation, vulnerability, and fear that accompany it. Therefore, a person is victimized "once" at the hands of his or her abuser and then over and over again emotionally and spiritually every time someone says, in so many words, "I don't believe you."

Second, to meet newly-disclosed cases of abuse with a different response, with positive responses, pastors can preach about the sin of abuse. Church leaders can obtain good videos on how to respond to disclosures of past or present abusive experiences. These videos can be shown at special open meetings called for the purpose of learning more about abuse. Ideally the videos would also be available for individuals to view confidentially, and there would be several staff people (or specific spiritually-mature members) who would be trained to handle cases of disclosure. It is important for a church to be prepared – before an abusive situation is ever disclosed. This preparation will help to create an atmosphere of safety for survivors. If a case has never been disclosed in your church, it could be a sign that survivors don't feel it would be safe to disclose; quite probably, there are hurting people right now in your congregation who yearn for someone to listen and believe, for compassion, and support.

Survivors did experience positive responses, however, such as positive verbal and physical support, use of Stephen Ministers when the pastor was too overwhelmed or not trained to deal with abuse issues, understanding of the concept of forgiveness and what are appropriate expectations for survivors, supportive sermons, counseling funds, removal of the offending pastor, and lovingkindness from church members. These and other positive and supportive responses are what the churches must substitute for initial denial to a survivor's story. First and foremost, we must listen and believe. Then we can help the survivor find whatever help she or he needs.

Feel the Pain and Understand the Full Effect of Abuse

The effects of abuse, we learned from survivors, are personal, extensive, devastating, deep, holistic, and long-term. Our effort at cataloging the effects identified by the survivors produced five broad categories: 1) increased fears and anxieties, which included nightmares, and fears of not being believed, of discovery, for life, and of continuing the cycle of abuse; 2) an altered sense of self and self esteem, as memories return or low self-esteem or multiple personalities develop; 3) church as an unsure foundation when they felt abandoned by God, mistrust in the church or altered perceptions of church-related imagery; 4) changes and constraints in behavior, as victims learn how to be abused with the least amount of pain, act out, run away, hide the "family secrets," or have problems in school; and 5) strained and loss of familial relationships. The consequences of abuse are many. A person may experience several at one time or a series of several over a long period of time.

It is important for those who are interacting with survivors to realize that these consequences can complicate and extend the healing process – and that "taking time" to heal is a good thing. Our society thrives on immediate results; but the healing of physical, emotional, and spiritual wounds takes time – time to acknowledge the hurt; time to grieve what has been lost or stolen or never will be; time to decide to give voice to their hurt; time to locate and trust others who can help them through the process; time to stumble and get back on the path to healing; and time to forgive self and others. Members of the church need to become more sensitive to both the immediate and the lasting effects of abuse. Becoming more sensitive to these issues will allow us, as members of the body of Christ, to minister healing, restoration, and reconciliation more effectively.

As the church becomes more sensitive to these issues, they will soon discover that even after some degree of "healing" is realized, some effects or consequences of the abuse remain for a lifetime and never disappear. Being "abused" acts as a master status, a condition through which one filters everything else, and even overshadows the status of "survivor." They will also begin to see how real the fear of becoming a person who abuses is for many survivors. Many of the survivors we interviewed stated that they knew that the person(s) who had abused them had also been abused; some could even go back a couple of generations. This is a fear that must be acknowledged and confronted by the church. In its teachings, counseling, or special programming, the church must insure that survivors understand that they can "choose" not to abuse others. The good news of the gospel is not only a message of salvation for tomorrow, it is also a message of the hope and reality of changed lives for today. In trying to counsel survivors, pastors should acknowledge their limitations and recognize when it may be appropriate for them to refer a survivor to another professional. Thus, pastors should investigate and create a list of ethical therapists, *before* the need arises. *be a networker*

The church must also see and treat abuse and its consequences as something involving more than individual survivors. As we mentioned in chapter 4, we all pay the high price of abuse. Clearly the ones who have been victimized pay the highest price and we do not intend nor desire to minimize their experience by stating that all people, abused or not, experience the consequences of abuse. When abuse is present within a congregation, the whole congregation suffers. If abusers are in positions of leadership and have not been removed from those positions (either for a time of restoration or permanently), then whatever areas of ministry they supervise are corrupted. If abusers are within the congregation at large and are not challenged to stop, they endanger the body and create a stumbling block for many in the body – a stumbling block that causes many to question (if not lose) their faith in God and the organized church. People who are neither survivors of abuse nor the abusers are also affected by abuse. These people are often the ones who are in close contact with survivors as relatives, friends, and co-workers. Many times these relationships are strained and broken without the nonabused/nonabuser person ever really understanding why. These people often question themselves to see if "it is just them" or is something "really" wrong. These may be the first persons to whom an abusive experience is exposed and they feel unsure about how to respond – often responding with disbelief, which is exactly what the survivor does not need. When survivors are hurting, we all *should* be hurting and working together toward healing and restoration. When we are not hurting, it means that our ministries are missing the mark. And if missing the mark in one area, one can only imagine in how many other areas we are deficient. When abuse is not dealt with within a congregation, we all pay. Making our congregations healthy communities requires members who are whole; toward that goal all congregations can work.

Don't Panic at Faith Questions

One of the deepest struggles for the abuse survivor is with God. The church must understand that simply asking "Why, God?" is vital to the survivor's inner healing, as vital as gaining an answer to the question. For even when God's existence is questioned, many survivors still express *wanting* to believe. And the difficulty of seeing God as "Father," a common struggle for the survivor, does not necessarily mean that the concept of God is rejected nor that God is not powerful. But when a child has been abused by his or her earthly father, it is difficult to speak lovingly of God, the Father. We must use more gender-free descriptives. Furthermore, we found that despite all that happened, many of our survivors stayed in the church, and few if any lost their faith in God. Most frequently, their faith took on a deeper sense of commitment. But for many, while the church rules and theology may have been threatening, "church" meant the people and their loving compassion. The church must learn not to panic when perhaps uncomfortable questions are asked by survivors. Understand that they are hurting and seeking answers crucial for their own survival, both spiritually and physically. Listening is the most helpful response.

The church, as we found out from the survivors we interviewed, while often acting as a hindrance to healing for survivors, *can* help in the healing process.

Explore Supportive Ventures

While survivors told about many ways in which the church failed to help, they also identified in their own words how they thought the church *could* help. The church needs to consider these suggestions very seriously and to explore ventures that will provide needed support for survivors in the churches' midst.

Recognize the Reality of Abuse. Accept that it happens, it happens in your own church, it happens in "good Christian families." Abuse is <u>not</u> a family issue. We are all God's children; He loans us to our parents for upbringing so we can then live according to His word. If those parents are not protecting His children, we need to do whatever we can to help.

Practice Accepting and Listening. Have programs which will teach members about the effects of abuse and how to respond, how to listen; include survivors to talk and answer questions, and other experts on the subject, such as therapists who deal with abuse issues; show videos.

Become Involved in the Healing of Survivors. Offer support groups; open your arms actively to include survivors in church activities – personally invite a hurting person individually; don't blame the victim; make the abuser responsible for his or her actions.

Make the Church a Safe Place. Creating an open and accepting atmosphere where the sin of abuse is preached from the pulpit and not tolerated by members is very healing.

Confront Abuse. Learn to recognize signs of abuse and be alert to it in all parishioners. Teach those signs to Sunday school teachers and others who interact with people in the church. Ask questions if something doesn't look quite right. Realize that abuse doesn't just happen once and usually doesn't happen to just one person; abusers don't stop without intervention of some sort, so confront the abuser and try to see to it that s/he gets help.

Demand Condemnation of What the Abuser has Done. Seek repentance from the abuser; make it known that you will not tolerate the actions, that as God's child he or she can change behavior with help and that is important to the abuser's salvation. Remove the offender from any church office or position of power.

Offer Healing Assistance to Abusers Who Repent. Offer them a safe place to come forward, a place where help will be offered and comfort given for their pain, but teach them that abusive actions are not okay. Recognize that abusers may have been victims of abuse themselves.

Help the Church Realize Ideal Qualities like being more accepting, open, supporting, sharing, and caring. This means being more accepting of everyone and not so judgmental. Be there to offer a supportive shoulder when needed; be willing to listen, yet keep confidences. The pastor would be compassionate and a good preacher. Keep in touch with the members and investigate what may seem to be problems; don't jump to conclusions. Recognize all gifts. Be a congregation of geese, not sea gulls.

References

The following references are given as a beginning place to learn more about the topic of abuse, how it affects its victims, and how the church can respond.

Books

Adams, Carol J. & Marie M. Fortune (Eds.) *Violence Against Women and Children: A Christian Theological Sourcebook.* New York: Continuum. 1995.

Anderson, Bill. *When Child Abuse Comes to the Church.* Minneapolis: Bethany House. 1992.

Berry, Jason. *Lead Us Not Into Temptation: Catholic Priests and the Sexual Abuse of Children.* New York: Doubleday. 1992.

Burroughs, Melba Graf. *The Road to Recovery: A Healing Journey for Survivors of Clergy Sexual Abuse.* Chatham, MA: Island Scribe. 1992.

Cohen, Barry M., Esther Giller & Lynn W. *Multiple Personality from the Inside Out.* Lutherville, MD: Sidran. 1991.

Daniels, April & Carol Scott. *Paperdolls: A True Story of Childhood Sexual Abuse in Mormon Neighborhoods.* San Diego: Recovery Publications, Inc. 1992.

Enroth, Ronald M. *Churches that Abuse.* Grand Rapids, MI: Zondervan. 1992

Feldmeth, JoAnn Ross & Midge Wallace Finley. *We Weep for Ourselves and Our Children: A Christian Guide for Survivors of Childhood Sexual Abuse.* San Francisco: HarperCollins. 1990.

Fortune, Marie M. *Sexual Abuse Prevention: A Study for Teenagers.* Cleveland: United Church Press. 1984.

_____. *Keeping the Faith: Questions and Answers for the Abused Woman.* San Francisco: HarperSanFrancisco. 1987.

_____. *Violence in the Family – a Workshop Curriculum for Clergy and Other Helpers.* Cleveland: The Pilgrim Press. 1991.

Friesen, James G. *The Truth about False Memory Syndrome.* Lafayette, LA: Huntington House Publishers. 1996.

Gelles, Richard J & Murray Straus. *Intimate Violence: The Causes and Consequences of Abuse in the American Family.* NY: Simon & Schuster. 1988.

Heggen, Carolyn H. *Sexual Abuse in Christian Homes and Churches.* Scottdale, PA: Herald Press. 1993.

Horton, Anne L. & Judith A. Williamson. (Eds.) *Abuse and Religion: When praying isn't enough.* Lexington, MA: D. C. Heath and Company. 1988.

Jansma, Theodore J. & Katharine St. Clair. *Becoming Kate: A Journey into the Life and the Healing of a Multiple Personality.* Santa Monica, CA: Roundtable Publishing Co. 1990.

MacDonald, Bonnie Glass. *Surely Heed Their Cry: A Presbyterian Guide to Child Abuse Prevention, Intervention, and Healing.* Louisville, KY: Presbyterian Church USA. 1993.

Mennonite Central Committee Domestic Violence Task Force. *Broken boundaries: Child Sexual Abuse.* Akron, PA: author. 1989.

————. *Purple Packet: Wife Abuse.* Akron, PA: author. 1987.

————. *Crossing the Boundary: Sexual Abuse by Professionals.* Akron, PA: author. 1990.

————. *Expanding the Circle of Caring: Ministering to the Family Members of Survivors and Perpetrators of Sexual Abuse.* Akron, PA: author. 1995.

————. *Lord Hear our Prayers: Domestic Violence Worship Resources.* Akron, PA: author. 1989.

Miller, Melissa A. *Family VIolence: The Compassionate Church Responds.* Scottdale, PA: Herald Press. 1994.

Parkinson, Patrick. *Child Sexual Abuse and the Churches.* United Kingdom: Hodder and Stoughton. 1997.

Pezdek, Kathy & William P. Banks. *The Recovered Memory/False Memory Debate.* San Diego: Academic Press, Inc. 1996.

Reid, K. G. & Marie M. Fortune. *Preventing Child Sexual Abuse, Ages 9-12.* Cleveland: United Church Press. 1989.

Reid, K. G. *Preventing Child Sexual Abuse, Ages 5-8.* Cleveland: United Church Press. 1994.

Sloat, Donald E. *The Dangers of Growing Up in a Christian Home.* Nashville, TN: Thomas Nelson, Inc. 1986.

————. *Growing Up Holy and Wholly: Understanding and Hope for Adult Children of Evangelicals.* Brentwood, TN: Wolgemuth & Hyatt, Publishers, Inc. 1990.

Stanko, Elizabeth. *Everyday Violence: How Women and Men Experience Sexual and Physical Danger.* London: Pandora Press. 1990.

Swagman, Beth A. *Too Close for Comfort: Understanding and Responding to the Reality of Abuse.* Grand Rapids, MI: CRC Publications. 1995.

Warshaw, Robin. *I Never Called it Rape.* New York: HarperCollins. 1994.

Videos
The following videos available are very good resources. Each of the sources may have additional videos or books and are excellent places to begin searching for helpful information.
    Mennonite Media Productions, 1251 Virginia Avenue, Harrisonburg, VA 22801.
    • "Beyond the news: Sexual abuse."

Center for the Prevention of Sexual and Domestic Violence, 936 North 34th Street, Suite 200, Seattle, WA 98103 USA.
- "Broken vows" Religious perspectives on domestic violence
- "Bless our children" Preventing sexual abuse
- "Hear their cries" Religious responses to child abuse
- "Not in my congregation" Prevention of clergy misconduct: Sexual abuse in the ministerial relationship
- "Wings like a dove" Healing for the abused Christian woman
- "To save a life" Ending domestic violence in Jewish families

Appendix A

The Survivors

As stated earlier, we could not reach all of our interviewees to obtain permission for inclusion in the book. Following are brief self descriptions of those who gave permission, as of the time of their interviews in the fall of 1992.

*Alyssa,*40, is married with children. She grew up in the Christian Reformed Church. She and her siblings received intense emotional rejection and physical beatings by their mother and also later by their father, both of whom considered themselves quite religious. Alyssa began her marriage with a wounded heart and a distorted view of family life, but with the help of a Christian counselor was finally able to begin healing. She always remembered her abuse and has been in counseling for seven years. She currently still attends a CRC congregation.

Anita is 63, married. She grew up in the Christian Reformed Church. Born with a congenital defect of the spinal column, she practiced walking after her parents relegated her to a wheelchair. Her mother subsequently physically and emotionally abused her for not listening to the Lord and staying in the wheelchair. Anita developed 26 multiple personalities and spent 13 years in therapy. She always remembered her abuse and still attends a Christian Reformed Church.

Anne is 45, married with children. She was brought up in and still attends the Christian Reformed Church. The family, except for her mentally-ill alcoholic mother, attended church twice most Sundays. She was sexually abused by her father, grandfather, uncle, a Christian School janitor, and a man she baby-sat for. The latter told her that Anne's mother told him to teach her what to do with boys. Her father sold her into pornography at a very young age, telling he had to do it to pay for her Christian School tuition; someone there told her she would be shot to death if she told. She repressed the abuse, but began having flashbacks when she went into therapy for being the "family caretaker."

Beatrice is 31, unmarried, and both working and going to school full time. She is one of eight children and grew up in the Christian Reformed Church. She was sexually abused by her father, an older brother, a minister friend of the family, a doctor and a teacher. She had repressed memories of the abuse until a psychologist treating her for the rejection of a broken engagement led her through age regression. She knew her father had also been abused as a child. Beatrice now attends a Reformed church.

Bonnie is 40 years old and grew up in the Christian Reformed Church. Her father sexually and physically abused her and her younger sisters. Her mother knew of the abuse but denied the charges and ignored Bonnie's cries for help. Bonnie became pregnant by her father and was taken to have an abortion. She was also sexually abused by a doctor. All memories of abuse were repressed until six years ago. She and her sister have cut off all communication with her family. She currently is in therapy and receives support from her pastor and the CRC. She has written a book about God's response to her hurt. It has not yet been published.

Brianna is 31, twice married and mother of four. One of six children, she grew up in the Christian Reformed Church. She was sexually and physically abused by her father. Her mother disbelieved the abuse because she believed that children are born into sin and can't be trusted. The sexual abuse stopped when Brianna refused to participate about age 13, but was replaced with verbal abuse. Her father was abused as a child by his father. Brianna always remembered her abuse. Two years after the interview, again divorced, she married a third time and joined a Congregational Church.

Charlene is 40 and married. Her sadistic father was part of an intergenerational satanic cult since his childhood and a multiple personality. He was very involved in the Baptist Church, taking his family to attend services twice on Sunday and once on Wednesday nights. He sometimes preached, and her mother, not a part of the satanism, taught Bible clubs. Because of her traumatic physical, emotional and sexual abuse by her father and other family and cult members, Charlene also became a multiple personality. She was also sexually abused by a college professor. She began therapy during college for depression and currently has been actively trying to heal for 4-1/2 years, four of them in therapy. Many of her memories surfaced first in the form of flashbacks. She is married to a minister and now attends a United Methodist Church.

Christy is 19, a single college student who is the oldest of four children. She grew up in the Mormon Church until she was removed from her home and placed in foster care after 9th grade because of her father's physical and sexual abuse. He was convicted and is currently in prison. She was also sexually abused for a short while by a brother who said, "If dad can do it, so can I." Her mother denies the abuse. Christy always remembered her abuse and currently attends an American Baptist church.

Edna, 45, was sexually abused by her great-uncle, who eventually went to jail on other child abuse charges. Although he lived nearby, her family never asked but rejoiced that he had "never touched any family members." Edna drank a bottle of perfume at age 6, trying to kill herself. She was brought up in the Catholic Church. She repressed and denied the abuse until seven years ago when she sought out healing for eating disorders and the abuse. She still attends the Catholic Church.

Elizabeth is 33, married with children. Her alcoholic father verbally abused all of his children, physically abused the two boys and sexually abused the two girls. Growing up, the family attended many churches, including Mennonite, Lutheran and Nazarene, moving when anyone in the church got too close. At age 10, Elizabeth told her father to stop the abuse or she would call the police. She repressed memories of the abuse until a teenaged date tried to go further than she desired; then the memories flooded back. She began counseling only when her marriage reached rock bottom years later, and began dealing with the abuse issues. She currently attends a Reformed Church in America congregation.

Emily, 37, is married with children and always has been in the Christian Reformed Church. Her parents, very controlling and demanding of perfection, physically and emotionally abused her. "I've lived most of my life to please my parents." The family attended church twice each Sunday and had devotions before meals. She and her sisters were also sexually abused by an older brother. She thought her home life was normal and didn't see it as abusive until after years of counseling which began because of her intense depression. Her pastor found the therapist and made the first appointment for her. She has been in therapy for 10 years.

Erica is 45, married with children. She grew up in a rural area and has always attended the Christian Reformed Church. She has been abused by three different people: 1) sexual abuse by an older brother who was very controlling; he later became a pastor. 2) a college instructor in Office Machines class would have an erection and lean against the females in class; and 3) emotional abuse by a pastor for whom she worked. She has always remembered the abuse, and attends a support group with others who worked for the abusive pastor. She also went through prayer therapy with a friend who conducted it.

Frank is 40. His family moved around a lot when he was a young child, often in southern states. His parents were Baptist. They divorced when he was 10 and he moved with his mother and his siblings to Michigan. Within a year his father committed suicide, an act which hit Frank very hard. He reacted by acting out, and running with a bad crowd. During junior high school he spent two summers on a farm. When the farmers asked him to live with them, his mother agreed. He went to a Baptist church while there and was sexually abused by its preacher who befriended him. Frank never forgot about the abuse and has been in counseling for six years, off and on. He now attends a Reformed Church of America congregation.

Heather is 58, married once, with children. She grew up in the Christian Reformed Church, attending twice weekly, and went to Christian schools. She was severely emotionally abused by her mother. Her father knew, but kept quiet because she wielded the power in the family (although he was "nominally the head of household"). She received the same kind of abuse from a Christian school teacher and, after marriage, from her husband. As a child, she escaped through reading, even though her mother told her it was sinful. Heather now attends the Reformed Church in America, although she takes the summer months off.

Holly is 35, married for the second time. She grew up in the Christian Reformed Church, attending twice each Sunday and going to Christian school. She was sexually abused by her father. She doesn't remember penetration, but does remember masturbating at age 4. At the time of her abuse, Holly's father was church clerk, the "head elder." Her mother denied that the abuse was anything serious. Holly was also physically abused by her first husband. She no longer attends church; she believes in God, but not in organized religion as she sees it.

Jane is 39, divorced. She graduated from Christian schools, attended the Christian Reformed Church twice weekly. Her strict father was an elder; he abused Jane both sexually and physically. Her mother knew something was going on but ignored it. Jane repressed memories of her abuse until about 6 years ago when she saw a Donahue show on abuse and incest; then memories began to return. She still attends the CRC.

Jessica is 45 years old, married with children and grandchildren. She grew up in a religious family which attended the Reformed Church. She was raped by her brother and his friends, physically and sexually abused by her parents and grandparents, sexually abused by both the minister and the janitor at her church. She has Dissociative Identity Disorder because of the severity of her abuse, "at least one" personality for each incident of abuse. She repressed memories of her abuse until six or seven years ago when she began having nightmares and flashbacks after a therapist she was seeing for depression asked if she had been abused as a child. Jessica has been in therapy for six years. She now attends the Christian Reformed Church.

Kayla is 39, divorced. She grew up in the Christian Reformed Church. She repressed memories of her abuse until an overweight, alcohol-abusing adult. She remembered being suicidal all her life, and when a massage therapist worked on the inside of her legs realized her father may have raped her as a child. She later had nightmares and flashbacks so began seeing a therapist and memories came back. She has been in therapy for 6 years. She no longer attends church but does attend Alcoholics Anonymous regularly.

Keith is 48, married with children. He grew up in Canada and attended the Christian Reformed Church. He was physically abused by his mother, who beat him with a "hunk of rubber hose." He was also sexually abused by an older brother, the family favorite because of his plans to become a minister; his parents denied the abuse. Keith still attends the Christian Reformed Church.

Kim is 40, married, the only daughter of alcoholic parents. She was sexually abused by her controlling father, who was the janitor at her Christian Reformed Church; she and her brothers were also physically and emotionally abused by both their parents. She has repressed memories of the first 24 years of life, including her abuse. She has been in therapy for over 20 years, first for depression and then memories of the abuse began to surface. People responded to her attempts at suicide by feeling sorry for her parents. Kim has many resentful feelings about the church and no longer attends.

Lacey is 41, married with children. Her parents involved at least three of their children, including Lacey, in Satanic rituals. She was also physically, emotionally, and severely sexually abused by both parents, who were actively involved in the Reformed Church. Her father was an elder for many years and her mother was involved in church groups. Lacey had repressed most of her abuse. She has been in therapy for six years and has been diagnosed with over 200 multiple personalities, several of whom came out during the interview. She now attends a Reformed Church and has had no contact with her family in four years.

Latoya is a 22 year college student who was first sexually abused by her uncle at age 4. When she was about 10, her brothers also began sexually abusing her. She was emotionally and physically abused by her father. Her sickly mother said she deserved it. When confronted as adults, her brothers said the activity was normal and she asked for it. Latoya attended Christian school and the Christian Reformed Church, where her father was an elder. She attempted suicide several times and was sent to secular psychiatrists, who blamed it on her father's religion. She quit going as soon as possible. She finally found a Christian counselor and has been in therapy 3-4 years. Her somewhat repressed memories began coming back in flashbacks. She now attends the Reformed Church of America.

Lydia is 42, married with children. One of five children, she was raised on a farm and attended the CRC. She and her siblings were physically abused by their rigid and strict father; the girls were also sexually abused. Her father told the children they were sinful and he was punishing them. She repressed her entire childhood, and began remembering the abuse when nightmares led her to see a therapist. She occasionally attend nondenominational churches, but does not associate herself with any particular church or denomination.

Maggie is 49, married, and was raised Catholic. She was sexually abused by her father and his brothers as a group and by her own brother, as well as by the priest who was principal of her school. She became suicidal in a sense, hoping she would be run over by a car and killed. Although she has always remembered the sexual abuse by her uncle when she was four years old, she remembers incidents here and there but still doesn't remember everything about the other abuse. "The memories are like photo snapshots, and what I want is a videotape." Maggie has been in therapy for 14 years off and on, and for five years intensively working on the abuse. She has been married more than once and her current husband doesn't want to be involved in church, which she says is probably part of the reason she picked him.

Martin is 36, married, with children. He grew up in the Roman Catholic church. He and his siblings were sexually abused by a

Catholic priest, who gave young boys alcohol and marijuana before molesting them. Martin's parents considered the priest to be family and often invited him to spend the night, giving him more opportunity to molest. Martin currently attends a Reformed Church in America congregation.

Maureen is 32. She grew up on a farm, attending the Christian Reformed Church. When she was 11 years old, she was raped by a hired hand at a neighboring farm. She became pregnant at 16, then married a man who verbally and physically abused her and allowed several members of his family to rape her. She was hospitalized several times because of his beatings, once losing a baby as a result of the abuse. She divorced after 15 months and has now remarried. She feels much anger and pain from her abuse. She suffers from Dissociative Identity Disorder. Some of the correspondence we had on this project came from another part of her. Maureen has always remembered the marital abuse, but not the pre-teen rape. She has been in therapy for about a year. She still attends the CRC.

Melissa is a married seminary student with children. She grew up in a mainline protestant church. Her parents were very religious and held very high expectations of her. She was sexually abused by her pastor when she tried to make plans for her wedding. After the abuse, she changed to another denomination. The abuse continued for nine years because she feared he would tell people she seduced him.

Michael is 41 years old, and was raised in the Christian Reformed Church. His family's multi-acre homestead was one of four on land originally owned by his grandfather. Beginning at age six, Michael was raped by someone regularly in one of the four houses. He thinks it was his grandfather, but can remember only the body and not the face of his abuser. He knows he told his mother about it and suspects grandfather was the only person she would cover up for as the family livelihood depended on him. She told him not to tell anyone or they couldn't go to church anymore. As a teenager he had repressed much of his experiences and suffered nightmares about being abused. Michael has not had any counseling to help him deal with his experiences, but has been trying to heal for 16 years. He now attends a Reformed church.

Monique is 45 years old and was raised with a Lutheran background. She is married for the second time and has children. Her son had been in therapy because of nightmares. The therapist asked her to take a psychological profile test, and later to read the book *The Courage to Heal*. After her 3-year-old daughter accused her son of sexual abuse, Monique began having "body memories." In one, her head began to hurt and then she had a "very clear memory" of her father throwing her back against the wall and sexually abusing her. She now has remembered that friends of her father also sexually abused her. She became pregnant, probably with her father's baby, when she was about 13; her father took her for an abortion. She has been in therapy for the abuse for two years. Today Monique no longer attends church.

Nicole is 30, married with children. Her parents were non-practicing Mennonites, who took the children to many churches, including Lutheran, Catholic, and Nazarene, but didn't attend themselves. Nicole was abused sexually, physically and emotionally by her alcoholic father; physically and emotionally by her mother; sexually by a grandfather. She attempted suicide as a child but those around her passed her attempts off as the stupid things children do. She always remembered at least some of the abuse but had some childhood memory lapses. Nicole is currently looking for a church home which preaches something she can believe in.

Robin is 47, married with children. She grew up Catholic and was forced into oral sex one time by her father when she was 12. After the priest laughed when she confessed that she had "committed adultery," she repressed the incident until she began having flashbacks and nightmares about it at age 35. She was also physically abused by an alcoholic husband (who currently claims to be in remission). She is not attending any church now but has not officially severed her ties with the Catholic Church.

Ryan is 30 years old and grew up in the Christian Reformed Church. He was one of four children and physically and emotionally abused by his father who taught him that he was unacceptable as a person. His father was very religious; Ryan refers to him as a "religious addict." Ryan is married now with children. His step-son was sexually abused by Ryan's wife's first husband, and the boy went on to sexually abuse Ryan's 3-year-old daughter. Ryan's brother is in prison for sexually abusing his own two sons. Ryan has never forgotten his abuse and has been in therapy for 2-1/2 years. He no longer attends church.

Sarah is 36 years old, and grew up in a relatively conservative community. She went to Catholic schools all through high school. She married at age 28 to a man she met at a Catholic singles group. She states, "I didn't know what a dysfunctional family was until I got married." Verbal abuse began right after the marriage; physical abuse came later. She stayed married for about 6 years, trying to make things work. She finally left her husband about 2 years ago, after he tried to strangle her several times and pointed a loaded shotgun at her. He also physically abused her children. Sarah has not repressed any of her experiences and although she is not in therapy now, she was for over a year. She is still a Catholic.

Appendix B

Schedule of Questions for Individual Interviews

[**Instructions**: begin tape record by saying "This is an interview with (ID#) on (date).]

1. **Interviewee background information** [Use for warmup, but this information is also important]
   - Tell me a little bit about who you are. You might begin with your gender and age, and then where you grew up.
   - Your church or denomination background would also be useful. What was it when you were growing up? What about now?

2. **Now I would like to hear your story of abuse, and where you are in your healing, if that is part of your story.** [Let interviewee tell story as a whole; if questions below not answered fully, then follow-up with them. Check off items as they are answered.]
   - Who was the abuser?
   - Do you know if the abuser was abused?
   - Did the abuser consider self a Christian?
   - Would people in your family consider the abuser Christian? How about people in your church? your community?
   - Whom did you tell? What was the reaction? Did your church know or suspect? How about your community?

3. **Describe your family when you were abused.**
   - Tell me about authority, control, and equality in that family. What role did religion play in these?

- What was the role of religion in family rules, e.g., rules about obeying parents, TV-watching on Sunday, self-expression, and making personal decisions?
- What was the relationship between spouses in that family?
- [If there was child abuse] what role did the non-offending parent play in the abuse, in its enactment, disclosure, treatment, and healing?
- What is that family like today?

4. **Was religion part of the abuse?**
   - Was religion used to justify the abuse?
   - Was religion a help or hindrance to your surviving abuse? to your healing?
   - Have your religious beliefs and faith been affected by your experience with abuse? In what ways?
   - Is God an ally or part of the problem?

5. **When you were abused, were you involved in any church or denomination?**
   - Was church involved in any way with your abuse?
   - How did people in church react to the abuse? How have Christians generally responded when told about your abuse?
   - What did you learn at church about women? about men? about the Bible? about your self-worth?
   - Did people in church give you any spiritual advice or help? What types?
   - Did you leave or consider leaving your church because of the abuse?
   - Did you seek out or join another church?
   - How do you feel about church today? about God?
   - Has church in any way been a source of healing for you?
   - How could a church minister better to survivors of abuse? How about to abusers?
   - Is there a support group for abuse survivors in your church? Would you attend one at your church, if one were available?

[Thank you very much for giving us this interview. You have been very helpful to the study.]

Endnotes

1. According to *Webster's New World Dictionary*, a concubine is a mistress; or a second wife of inferior social and legal status. (p. 289)

2. Trible, Phyllis. *Texts of terror: Literary-feminist readings of Biblical narratives.* Philadelphia: Fortress Press. 1984. P. 79.

3. Kemp, C. Henry, Frederic N. Silverman, Brandt F. Steele, William Droegemueller and Henry K. Silver. 1962. "The Battered Child Syndrome." *Journal of the American Medical Association* 181: 17-24.

4. Gelles, Richard J. "Family Violence." *Annual Review of Sociology* 11: 347-367. Palo Alto, CA: Annual Reviews, Inc. 1985.

5. Straus, Murray A. "Foreword" pp 13-17 in Richard J. Gelles *The Violent Home: A Study of Physical Aggression between Husbands and Wives.* Beverly Hills, CA: Sage. 1974.

6. Star, Barbara. "Patterns of Family Violence." Social Casework: The Journal of Contemporary Social Work: 339-346.

7. Brassard, Maria R. , Robert Germain and Stuart N. Hart. *Psychological Maltreatment of Children and Youth.* p. 3. Elmsford, NY: Pergamon Press. 1987

8. Turbett, J. Patrick and Richard O'Toole. "Physicians' Recognition of Child Abuse." Presented at Annual Meeting of American Sociological Association, New York. 1980.

9. Rice, Rodger R. and Ann W. Annis. A Survey of Abuse in the Christian Reformed Church. Grand Rapids, MI: Calvin College Social Research Center, 1991.

10. Bass, Ellen and Laura Davis. *The Courage to Heal: A Guide for Women Survivors of Child Sexual Abuse.* New York: Harper & Row, Publishers, Perennial Library. 1988.

11. Goodman, Gail S. et al. "Predictors of Accurate and Inaccurate Memories of Traumatic Events Experienced in Childhood" in Pezdek, K and Banks, W. P. (Eds). *The Recovered Memory/False Memory Debate.* San Diego: Academic Press. Pp 3-28. 1996.

12. Harvey, Mary R. and Judith Lewis Herman. "Amnesia, Partial Amnesia, and Delayed Recall among Adult Survivors of Childhood Trauma" in Pezdek, Kathy and William P. Banks (Eds) . *The Recovered Memory/False Memory Debate.* San Diego: Academic Press. Pp 29-40. 1996

13. "Interim Report of the Working Group on Investigation of Memories of Childhood Abuse" in Pezdek, Kathy and William P. Banks (Eds). *The Recovered Memory/False Memory Debate.* San Diego: Academic Press. Pp 371-372. 1996.

14. Myers, David G. *Psychology* (5th edition). New York: Worth Publishers. P. 300. 1998

15. Rice, Rodger R. and Ann W. Annis. A Survey of Abuse in the Christian Reformed Church. Grand Rapids, MI: Calvin College Social Research Center, 1991.

16. This is also found in Exodus 20: 12. (*Honor your father and your mother, so that you may live long in the land the Lord is giving you.*)

17. Keene, Frederick W., "The Politics of Forgiveness." On The Issues, Vol IV, No. 4, Fall 1995, pp. 32-35.

Index

abuse
  biblical accounts of rape, 1-2
  of children, 2-5, 22-26
    see also survivors' stories
  denial of, 123
  effects of
    acting out, 57-58, 61-62
    avoidance behavior, 62, 63
    church no longer a comfort,
      53-56
    compartmentalized memory,
      49-50
    consequences beyond
      survivors, 124
    Dissociative Identity
      Disorder, 13, 15, 49-50
    family secrets, 59-60
    fears and anxieties, 44-47
    isolation from friends, 66
    low self-esteem, 12, 14, 50-
      52
    not seeking professional
      help, 61
    poor academic performance,
      64
    sexual difficulties, 58
    strained family relations, 65-
      71
  in good Christian families, 5, 7,
    10, 22-24

  learning how to be abused, 56
  by pastors, 10, 24-26
  scriptural justification, 10-13
    see also scripture references
  of spouse, 3, 4
    see also survivors' stories
abusers
  the church as, 109
  healing provided for, 99-102
  references to, 1, 9-26
    see also survivors' stories
  removal from church, 42, 43
  as victims, 110
abusive family members, 68-71
academic performances, 64
American Psychological
  Association, 4
battered child syndrome, 2
child abuse recognized as social
  problem, 2
Christian, definition of, 40
church
  accepting survivors, 97-99
  as a safe place, 89-93, 102-105,
    120-123
  and negative responses to abuse,
    8-35
  and positive responses to abuse,
    35-42, 121-124
  confronting abuse, 105-107

Scripture Index